Joy in the Battle

Joy
in the
Battle

Mary Sorrentino

ATLANTA, GEORGIA

Published in Atlanta, Georgia by Joy on Purpose.

ISBN: 978-0-9973328-0-3

Library of Congress Control Number: 2016906481

To Paul, Sarah, and Ted

My prayer for you, my precious family, is that each of you will discover the unparalleled JOY of experiencing God's victory every day of your life.

For the LORD your God is the one who goes with you to fight for you against your enemies to give you victory.   Deuteronomy 20:4

Contents

Acknowledgements

I owe a debt of gratitude to so many for their part in making this book a reality. First and foremost, thanks go to my husband Paul, for his patience, his willingness to be a first and last editor, his wonderful wit and creative ideas, and mostly for his unconditional love in a long journey. I am also so grateful to my daughter Sarah Noble. Without her creative genius, the cover of this book would not be the beautiful design that it is.

And to my editor, Jane Hoppe, I am thankful for all her help, not only in lending her expertise and eye for all the detail that I so easily skim past, but even more, for her thoughtful ideas and commentary on content, as well as her contributions and illustrations. Jane's deep spiritual sensitivity and devotion to God helped make this work biblically sound and hopefully, pleasing to our Lord.

I would also like to thank Sheree DeCouto, who believed in both my writing and speaking skills even when I didn't, and has given me the opportunity to spread my wings through the women's ministry at Fellowship Bible Church. I am also eternally grateful to all the women who have trusted me to walk alongside them on their journeys with God, through coaching, teaching and Bible studies. Without sharing in their experiences and struggles, *Joy in the Battle* would never have become a reality.

Finally, I want to thank my sweet Savior for the privilege of being used in His service. The honor and amazement I feel at being used to teach God's truth is more than I can express.

Introduction

For our struggle is not against flesh and blood ...
Ephesians 6:12

I am continually amazed by how frequently God's plans take us in a direction we never could have dreamed or imagined. (1 Corinthians 2:9) In my own life, God has taken me from the world of corporate information technology to the new and exciting adventure of Professional Life Coaching, writing and speaking. Who would have thought? The truth is I never planned to write a book on spiritual warfare, although for many years God had been nudging me to write on the subject I've been passionate about most of my adult life – finding God's *joy* in the midst of life's most difficult circumstances. But with a passion for joy, why in the world would I write a book on this topic?

At every turn, I meet Christian men and women who find it almost impossible to sustain joy. In my book called *Joy on Purpose*, I explored how we can intentionally find joy in the midst of life's difficulties. One key principle taught in the book is to never forget we are in a spiritual battle.

As followers of Christ, we have an enemy who seeks to steal our joy and separate us from the One who saves us and gives our lives meaning and hope. (John 10:10) After sharing the chapter on "The Battle" with a number of women's groups, I realized that most of us are not armed for battle. Not only do we fail to fully grasp the Bible's teaching on the war raging between the powers of God and Satan, but many don't really understand, or possibly don't believe, that there truly is another dimension – a parallel world existing outside what we can see, hear and touch. (Ephesians 6:12) But we certainly do feel its effects. Week after week, month after month, women told me of the struggles they experience in their lives and asked, "Do you think this is spiritual warfare?"

My answer to their question was, "Perhaps it is. What do you know about the topic?" And far too many replied, "Not much." Although most were Christians for many years, they were novices in the fine art of battle. And if you asked, most of them would tell you they are pretty uncomfortable with the whole idea of being a soldier for Christ. It is not a role we really want to play. But the Bible says, as followers of Christ we have made an enemy for ourselves and have joined God's army, whether we planned to do so or not. Hmmm … there's that planning idea again! God's plan for us is often different from our own. But the good news is, as warriors in this cosmic battle, God has given us everything we need to fight and win against our enemy, Satan.

I confess I have asked myself and God over and over again, "Who am I to write a study on spiritual warfare? I'm not a pastor or theologian." Many books and studies have been written on this topic and the last thing I wanted to do was re-create the wheel. So I began to dig and study and research. I found that there are, in fact, many extremely good studies and books on spiritual warfare, including *Lord, Is It Warfare? Teach Me to Stand* by Kay Arthur, *The Battlefield of the Mind* by Joyce Meyer, *The Invisible War* by Chip Ingram and *The Bondage Breaker* by Neil Anderson.

But none of these directly addressed the passion God has placed on my heart, the core of my ministry and the question on the hearts of the women I spoke to about our spiritual war. None of these books asked the question, "How do I find joy in the midst of this battle?" So after many months of deep prayer, and hour upon hour of research, I finally realized I could not say *no* to the Almighty, even if I was a bit nervous about putting myself on the front lines of war. The battle is the Lord's, and He has asked this soldier to fight with pen in hand.

The book you're about to read is truly a work of obedience. In it, with God's constant help and the truth of His Word as our compass, we will tackle this tough topic and ask the question, "How do I find joy when a war rages around me?" Before we begin, however, let me say just a word about joy. Our goal in this, or any other *Joy on Purpose* book, is not to find happiness or prosperity. God's Word doesn't promise us either, at least not within the material or earthly context that we would expect. But it has so much to say about *joy* – real *inner joy* that comes from having an intimate relationship with the God who created and saved us. This joy runs so deep that no matter what our external circumstances, it cannot be taken away – not by people, not by events and not even by Satan himself. That is the joy we want to find and keep through all the battles of our lives. The enemy comes to steal, kill and destroy. But God promises us peace, life and yes, even joy! (John 10:10; John 16:33; John 15:11)

Thank you for joining me on this exciting and challenging adventure. Together let's discover how to arm ourselves for the spiritual battles we inevitably face as believers in Jesus Christ, and hold tight to the One who *is* our armor, our protector and our joy.

> Finally be strong in the Lord and in his mighty power. Put on the full armor of God, so that you can take your stand against the devil's schemes. For our struggle is not against flesh and blood, but against the rulers, against the authorities, against the powers of this dark world and against the spiritual forces of evil in the heavenly realms. Therefore put on the full armor

of God, so that when the day of evil comes, you
may be able to stand your ground, and after you
have done everything, to stand.
(Ephesians 6:10–13)

1

An Invisible World

*There is a visible and an invisible world
that intersect, and we live in the intersection.*
Chip Ingram[1]

What Happened to My Joy?

Have you ever known a person who seemed to be
continuously filled with joy? It's hard to think of anyone
like that, isn't it? Most of us try very hard to be positive,
to look at the glass as half-full instead of half-empty. But
it is difficult to maintain that kind of attitude. Bad things
happen. Our "luck" runs out. We deal with illness or the
loss of a job or dysfunctional family relationships and *poof*
– there goes our joy. We fight to keep ourselves from
becoming depressed, or we struggle to maintain positive
thoughts about those we love or others in our lives. It's a
roller coaster of emotions. Why does it seem so hard to
hold on to joy?

Perhaps part of the problem is we're confusing joy with happiness. Are they the same? Can you have joy even when the circumstances of life make you unhappy? And how do you cling to joy when things go wrong, people disappoint you, or life just seems way too tough to manage? Our minds tend to spiral into negative thinking far too quickly, frequently running down a path of bitterness, anger and even despair. Truly, there is a significant difference between happiness and joy. This is what the New Bible Dictionary says about joy:

> In both the Old Testament and New Testament, joy is consistently the mark both individually of the believer, and corporately of the church. It is a quality, and not simply an emotion, grounded upon God Himself and indeed derived from Him (Psalm 16:11; Philippians 4:4; Romans 15:13), which characterizes the Christian's life on earth (1 Peter 1:8), and also anticipates the joy of being with Christ forever in the kingdom of heaven (Revelation 19:7).[2]

Did you get that? "Joy is… a quality, and not simply an emotion, grounded upon God Himself…" No wonder God's Word speaks far more often about joy than happiness. The Hebrew words translated as "happy" are used twenty-nine times in the New International Version of the Bible. But the Greek and Hebrew words translated as "joy" are used two hundred forty-seven times. Why? I believe it is because God *promises* us joy. He does not tell us we'll be happy or that we won't have trouble in our lives. Quite the opposite is true. In the gospel of John, Jesus tells us, "… In this world you will have trouble. But take heart! I have overcome the world." (John 16:33)

We can be sure that trouble will always be part of our lives here on this earth. But God's Word promises, encourages and even celebrates the *joy of the Lord!* (Nehemiah 8:10) If that is true, why is it so hard to stay joy-filled? Why are we so quick to think negative thoughts and allow our hearts and minds to be torn away from the truth and from the only One who brings us joy?

It's a Battle

God's Word tells us over and over again, that we have an enemy who would love to *kill* our spirits, *steal* our joy, and *destroy* our relationship with God and each other. (John 10:10) The moment we chose to become followers of Christ, whether we were aware of it or not, we enlisted in God's army. As believers we are now enemies of Satan. His mission is to destroy his enemies, and the battlefield where he does much of his destructive work is in our minds. (Romans12:2) Have you ever found yourself thinking a negative, or perhaps even an evil thought, when suddenly you say to yourself, "Where in the world did *that* come from?" Do you ever catch your thoughts running down a slippery slope of negativism, or even anger or hate, and then realize this mindset just *happened* without consciously choosing to dwell on these kinds of thoughts?

I have to admit, I do. And so did one of my coaching clients. We'll call her Sara. Sara is a Christian woman who is passionately pursuing God and the restoration of her marriage, which was on the brink of divorce. She has purposely chosen to love her husband God's way and has decided not to give up even though most of her friends, even Christian friends, and family have been telling her to end their marriage of seven years. But God is so much bigger than any of our problems. He has given Sara some amazing miracles in the last year, and her marriage relationship, although not totally restored, is in a place that would have seemed impossible just a year ago.

However, in a recent coaching session, as Sara shared how well things were going in her relationship, she also spoke of how her mind keeps going back to the time when she was terribly hurt and angry at her husband. Just when she begins thinking about the changes in her husband and their strengthening marriage, she suddenly finds herself thinking, "Yes, but remember when he did this …?" The old feelings of anger well up within her for offenses that were forgiven and healed long ago, offenses she thought were long forgotten.

What keeps drawing Sara's mind back to closed chapters? What makes her keep thinking about things her husband did wrong, even though both of them have changed so dramatically in the past year? I believe there is a war taking place on the battlefield of Sara's mind. The enemy surely does not want this marriage and family to be restored and to honor God. Satan loves nothing more than to destroy marriages and families, leaving children with broken homes, and painting a picture for the whole world to see of yet another failure of this God-created institution.

So, once again Sara and I talked about *living in the truth*. We spoke about the importance of not allowing the enemy to take her mind back to a place God had healed long ago. The truth is this marriage is on its way to restoration by the grace and power of a mighty God. And the enemy's schemes to draw Sara back into anger and pain of the past will not work, as long as she stands firm in the truth and power of God.

Many of us are like Sara. The enemy plants seeds of doubt, fear, anger, envy and a host of others in our minds to pull us away from God and victory. Our Father in heaven warned us in His Word that Satan will use his most clever schemes to lie, twist the truth, manipulate and deceive us. And many of those schemes take place in the mind. The joy we seek so much to keep is undermined when we allow ourselves to be deceived by the enemy's lies, instead of holding steadfastly to the truth. Real joy, the joy that comes from our intimate relationship with our Creator, can't be taken away from us by anyone or anything. But if Satan can make us believe his lies, he has accomplished his purpose. He can hide the joy of the Lord so well in deception and twisted thinking that, although we are children of the King, we act like spiritual paupers, living under the bondage of his lies instead of walking in the power and victory that is ours as God's own children.

That is the battle. It takes place twenty-four hours a day, seven days a week in every country, every city, every home and every mind across the entire world. Our purpose in this book is to learn how to recognize the enemy's lies, cover ourselves in God's armor, and stand firm so that no one and nothing can steal the joy that God *promises* in our relationship with Christ. But before we can learn how to recognize Satan's schemes and lies, it's important that we first talk about the reality of this invisible battle and the unseen world in which the war takes place.

Two Worlds

Let's play a game. How many things can you name that are invisible to our senses, yet are as real as this page? As time marches on, science has given us the ability to know and understand more and more about our physical world.

We have uncovered the mysteries of worlds that are completely undetectable to our human senses – the distant galaxies, the intricate design of the atom, and even something as simple (or perhaps I should say as complex) as air itself. We know it's there. We breathe it. We need it to exist, and yet, have you ever *seen* air? Actually, when I lived in southern California, I thought I could see the air as I drove down the freeway and saw the thick brown blanket of haze hanging over the city. Of course, I wasn't really seeing the air. It was the muck we humans had spewed into it that made it visible to my eyes and even perceptible to my sense of smell. The air itself remained invisible. What else do you know for certain is real, even though you can't see, feel or touch it?

So, with the scientific *reality* of an invisible world all around us, why is it so hard to believe the spiritual realm is just as real as what we see, and don't see? The Bible tells us this invisible spiritual world is in fact, very real. For example, in the book of Daniel the angel Gabriel appeared to Daniel and encouraged him not to be afraid. Gabriel told him why there was a delay in God's answer to his prayer.

> Do not be afraid, Daniel. Since the first day that you set your mind to gain understanding and to humble yourself before your God, your words were heard, and I have come in response to them. But the prince of the Persian kingdom

resisted me twenty-one days. Then Michael, one of the chief princes, came to help me, because I was detained there with the king of Persia. Now I have come to explain to you what will happen to your people in the future, for the vision concerns a time yet to come. (Daniel 10:13–14)

The Bible Knowledge Commentary explains Daniel 10:13-14 this way: "When Daniel first began fasting and mourning in response to the vision of a great war, God had dispatched the angel Gabriel with a message for him, but Gabriel was hindered by the 'prince of the Persian kingdom.' Since men cannot fight with angels... the prince referred to here must have been a satanic adversary."[3]

In the three years that Christ ministered here on earth before His death and resurrection, Jesus himself frequently spoke of and interacted with the kingdom of the enemy. In the gospel of John, we see Jesus talking to a group of Jews who are questioning where His power came from. He says to them:

Why is my language not clear to you? Because you are unable to hear what I say. You belong to your father, the devil, and you want to carry out your father's desire. He was a murderer from the beginning, not holding to the truth, for there is no truth in him. When he lies, he speaks his native language, for he is a liar and the father of lies. (John 8:43–44)

It's quite obvious that to Jesus, the invisible world and His enemy, the devil, are without a doubt very real. And He clearly knows His adversary. Jesus had many interactions with Satan's army as well. In the fifth chapter of Mark, Jesus speaks directly to the demons, or *"evil spirits."*

> They went across the lake to the region of the Gerasenes. When Jesus got out of the boat, a man with an evil spirit came from the tombs to meet him. This man lived in the tombs, and no one could bind him anymore, not even with a chain. For he had often been chained hand and foot, but he tore the chains apart and broke the irons on his feet. No one was strong enough to subdue him. Night and day among the tombs and in the hills he would cry out and cut himself with stones.

> When he saw Jesus from a distance, he ran and fell on his knees in front of him. He shouted at the top of his voice, "What do you want with me, Jesus, Son of the Most High God? In God's name don't torture me!" For Jesus had said to him, "Come out of this man, you evil spirit!"

> Then Jesus asked him, "What is your name?"
> "My name is Legion," he replied, "for we are
> many." And he begged Jesus again and again not
> to send them out of the area. (Mark 5:1–10)

In what is probably Jesus' most famous interaction
with the kingdom of darkness, we read the details of His
temptation in the desert by Satan recorded in the gospels
of both Matthew and Luke. (See Matthew 4:1–11; Luke
4:1–13) Read these accounts for yourself, and be sure to
take note of how Jesus fights the lies of His enemy. Over
and over again He declares "*It is written ...*" Jesus himself
fights Satan's lies with the truth of God's Word.

Know Your Enemy

The Bible is clear. The spiritual world is very real and a
cosmic war is being fought there, a war with eternal
consequences. This battle is being waged for the heart,
soul, mind and life of every human being who ever lived
or will live. As in any battle or competition, the key to
winning is to know your opponent. Know his strategy,
strengths and weaknesses, and know your own strengths
and weaknesses as well. In Chapter Two we will look
more closely at our strength and power in Christ and at
the strategies and tactics of our enemy. But first, let's
examine who our enemy is and how he works in this

world. In *The Bible Exposition Commentary*, Warren Wiersbe says this about Satan:

> Who is Satan? The enemy has many different names. Devil means "accuser." The Bible tells us he accuses God's people day and night before the throne of God (Revelation 12:7–11). Satan means "adversary." He is the enemy of God. He is also called the tempter (Matthew 4:3), the murderer and the liar (John 8:44). He is compared to a lion (1 Peter 5:8), a serpent (Genesis 3:1; Revelation 12:9), and an angel of light (2 Corinthians 11:13–15). He is called "the god of this age" (2 Corinthians 4:4). Where did he come from, this spirit-creature that seeks to oppose God and defeat His work? Many people believe that in the original Creation, he was "Lucifer, son of the morning" (Isaiah 14:12–15) and that he was cast down because of his pride and his desire to occupy God's throne.
>
> Many mysteries are connected with the origin of Satan, but what he is doing and where he is going is certainly no mystery. Since he is a created being, and not eternal as God is, he is limited in his knowledge and activity. Unlike God, Satan is not all-knowing, all-powerful, or everywhere-present. Then how does he accom-

plish so much in so many different parts of the world? The answer is in his organized helpers.[4]

Satan works in our world through people and through his private army of spiritual beings, fallen angels that are often called demons.

Satan Works Through People

Wow! Can that be true? Does our enemy really work through people here on earth? Jesus Himself said, "He who is not with me is against me." (Matthew 12:30) When you think about the depravity of this world since the fall of Adam, it seems pretty evident that the *prince of this world* is using many who are not "with God" to accomplish his destructive and evil purposes. Those who don't follow God, whether they are an evil, depraved lunatic like Adolf Hitler, or simply someone who does not listen to the Spirit of God, all are in fact capable of becoming pawns in a very important war game. The most well-known example in Scripture is Judas Iscariot, who betrayed Jesus.

> Then Satan entered Judas, called Iscariot, one of the Twelve. And Judas went to the chief priests and the officers of the temple guard and discussed with them how he might betray Jesus. (Luke 22:3–4)

And there are many other biblical examples including the story of the sorcerer Elymas in the book of Acts.

> But Elymas the sorcerer (for that is what his name means) opposed them and tried to turn the proconsul from the faith. Then Saul, who was also called Paul, filled with the Holy Spirit, looked straight at Elymas and said, "You are a child of the devil and an enemy of everything that is right! You are full of all kinds of deceit and trickery. Will you never stop perverting the right ways of the Lord?" (Acts 13:8–10)

It is apparent that the enemy can use those who turn their backs on God like Judas and Elymas the sorcerer or other evil individuals like Hitler but what about regular people? Can the enemy use even a Christian for his purposes? Yes. Satan does use people every day who make choices in their lives that don't honor God, from what they watch on television to how they treat others. Many biblical examples demonstrate that Satan can and does use even believers in his schemes when we are not armed with the truth. Think about our Lord's response to Peter after he told Jesus he would never allow Him to suffer and die.

> From that time on Jesus began to explain to his disciples that he must go to Jerusalem and suffer

many things at the hands of the elders, chief priests and teachers of the law, and that he must be killed and on the third day be raised to life. Peter took him aside and began to rebuke him. "Never, Lord!" he said. "This shall never happen to you!" Jesus turned and said to Peter, "Get behind me, Satan! You are a stumbling block to me; you do not have in mind the things of God, but the things of men."
(Matthew 16:21–23)

If Satan could use Peter, who walked with Jesus in the flesh every day, surely we must be alert. (1 Peter 5:8) We must arm ourselves for the battle. Arm yourself with truth. *Live* in the truth. Put on the *full armor of God* and never take it off. (Ephesians 6:11) We will spend the majority of our time in this book learning how to do just that.

Satan Works Through Demons

Satan's army is not made up solely of human beings. He also works through his spiritual agents – fallen angels, or demons. The Bible teaches that when Satan rebelled and fell from heaven, he took many of the angelic host with him.

> And there was war in heaven. Michael and his angels fought against the dragon, and the dragon and his angels fought back. But he was not strong enough, and they lost their place in heaven. The great dragon was hurled down – that ancient serpent called the devil, or Satan, who leads the whole world astray. He was hurled to the earth, and his angels with him.
> (Revelation 12:7–9)

Those fallen angels chose to follow Satan and honor him over God. According to the Bible, our one and only source for God's truth, this army of spiritual agents will be employed full-time doing Satan's work until they are destroyed along with Satan himself at the end of time.

> Then he will say to those on his left, "Depart from me, you who are cursed, into the eternal fire prepared for the devil and his angels."
> (Matthew 25:41)

How important are demons in the enemy's strategy and schemes? There are more than eighty references to demons or demon possession in the Word of God. That should tell us these fallen angels are alive and very active in the invisible world. Do we need to be afraid of them? No! Jesus has power over *every power and authority,* (Colossians 2:10) and as believers we stand *in Christ*

(John 17:26) and have His power and authority to resist the enemy and his army.

> For I am convinced that neither death nor life, neither angels nor demons, neither the present nor the future, nor any powers, neither height nor depth, nor anything else in all creation, will be able to separate us from the love of God that is in Christ Jesus our Lord. (Romans 8:38–39)

Our Battle Strategy

Before we finish this first leg of our journey to finding *Joy in the Battle*, it's important that we talk a little about how we will fight this war. In any battle or competition, the best way to fight is to know your opponent's strategy. In his book, *The Invisible War*, Chip Ingram writes,

> It's Super Bowl Sunday, and both teams are ready. They have dreamed about this all season, but the last two weeks they've done a lot more than dream. They have watched films. Hour after hour after hour they've sat in front of a screen, clicking the remote to speed the film forward, pressing it to rewind it back a few seconds, watching their opponent's plays over and over again ... They know the opposition. They have learned the schemes ... They have spent some of their time running drills, but they

have spent more time on their homework. There will be no surprises because they've done the math. Why? Because they want to win. [5]

The Bible tells us everything we need to know about how our enemy fights this war. We'll discuss Satan's methods and schemes in more detail in Chapter Two, but for now let's look at some of what God's Word reveals to us about his methods.

- ❖ He is a liar. (John 8:44)
- ❖ He accuses believers. (Revelation 12:10)
- ❖ He misuses Scripture. (Matthew 4:6; Luke 4:10)
- ❖ He is a deceiver. (2 Corinthians 11:14)
- ❖ He tempts Christians to fall away. (Luke 22:31)
- ❖ He blinds unbelievers. (2 Corinthians 4:4)

These are just a few of the methods used by Satan in his attempt to defeat God's children. No wonder God's Word warns us to stay alert. (1 Peter 5:8) But, let's not make the mistake of attributing more power to the enemy than he actually has, or see demons around every corner. Instead, let's celebrate the *truth* that our enemy is a defeated foe!

- ❖ Christ's death and resurrection defeated Satan. (Hebrews 2:14–15)

- ❖ Jesus Christ is stronger than the enemy. (John 14:30)
- ❖ Jesus Christ's name is powerful against Satan. (Luke 10:17)
- ❖ Satan's power is limited. (Job 1:12)
- ❖ God protects people from the enemy. (2 Thessalonians 3:3)
- ❖ Christians can resist Satan. (James 4:7)
- ❖ Christians can overcome Satan. (1 John 2:13–14)
- ❖ Satan cannot separate us from God. (Romans 8:38–39)
- ❖ The enemy and his agents will be destroyed. (Revelation 17:14)
- ❖ Satan's final destiny is sealed. (Revelation 20:1–3, 10)

We have taken some important first steps in our journey to find *Joy in the Battle*. Joy is ours through the intimate and incredible relationship God wants to have with each and every one of us. Yes, we have an enemy who would like to stop us and steal our joy, but thank God, in His great love and mercy He has given us all we need for victory – His armor for the battle. Here is our strategy:

- ❖ Know your enemy and his schemes.
- ❖ Know your position and your strength in Christ.

❖ Know the truth so well that you recognize the enemy's lies.

❖ Put on God's armor and stand *in* Christ.

In Christ's fervent prayer to His Father in John 17:17, He prayed for you and for me, saying "Sanctify them by the truth; your word is truth." Don't ever forget how Jesus fought back when Satan lied to Him in the desert. (Matthew 4:1–22; Luke 4:1–13) Jesus counteracted Satan's lies with truth. He said "It is written … It is written … It is written …" If Jesus Himself fought the enemy's attacks with Scripture, what better way for us to experience the joy of victory in our own battles, than by fighting back the same way Christ did? The enemy flees where truth and the name of Jesus abound.

At the end of each chapter you will find a *Key Takeaway* to help you hold on to what you learned, a *Memory Verse* to fight the enemy the same way Christ did, and *Study Questions* for individual or group study to help you dig more deeply into God's Word. I strongly encourage you to use these resources to build up your spiritual arsenal. We are at war, but you already have all you need to win.

An Invisible World – Reflections

Key Takeaway:

The moment we chose to become followers of Christ, whether we were aware of it or not, we enlisted in God's army.

Memory Verse:

"But the Lord is faithful, and he will strengthen you and protect you from the evil one."

(2 Thessalonians 3:3)

Notes:

An Invisible World – Study Questions

1. Do you ever feel as if there is a battle going on in *your* mind? How do you fight your battle?

2. Read Philippians 4:8. The word used in this passage for "think about" is the Greek term *logizomai* which means to reason about, or ponder. What does *how you think* have to do with holding on to God's promise of joy?

3. Read John 8:44 and 1 John 2:20–21. What do these verses tell you about how the enemy works and how to fight back?

4. In Revelation 12:10 the enemy is referred to as "the accuser of the brethren." How does Satan accuse you? How will you respond the next time the enemy whispers accusations in your ear?

5. In 1 John 3:8, we are told, "The reason the Son of God appeared was to destroy the devil's work." How do you feel about continuing to fight battles, even though Christ defeated Satan at the cross?

6. Read 2 Peter 3:9. What does it tell you about why the battles continue?

2

Standing in Christ

Therefore put on the full armor of God, so that
when the day of evil comes, you may be able
to stand your ground, and after you have
done everything, to stand.
Ephesians 6:13

Children of the King

Our battle against the powers of darkness is real. I'm
fighting it even as I write the words on this page. The
enemy is putting negative, angry, even destructive
thoughts in my mind, which translate into similar harmful
feelings. Why? The answer is, quite simply, because he
knows my weaknesses and my struggles, and because he
can.

The battleground of the mind is fertile ground for
Satan's seeds of destruction. When he sees an opportunity, he seizes it and builds on it, often whispering lies
that tear down instead of build up. Satan is a student of
our lives. He watches our every move, and he knows our

weaknesses, our mistakes, our difficult relationships, our trials and our pain. He uses anything and everything we experience in an all-out attempt to make his lies sound like truth and to pull us away from our God and from each other.

But we are children of the King! We are forgiven, forever. We can take every thought captive to Christ (1 Corinthians 10:5) and choose to think on things that are good and true and praiseworthy. (Philippians 4:8) And when we do, when we ask God to take control of our minds, and we choose to speak *and think* only the truth – the enemy's lies no longer have any power. Oh yes, this spiritual war is very real, and the one we fight against is a master deceiver, the father of lies. "When he lies, he speaks his native language, for he is a liar and the father of lies." (John 8:44) He uses schemes, trickery and methods that can take down kings and kingdoms. But the truth is: Satan is defeated. His power over us was broken at the cross of Christ. But, if Satan is defeated, why do our battles continue?

On June 6, 1944, *D-Day*, the United States and Allied troops landed on the beach in Normandy, France, beginning a bloody battle that will long be remembered as the *turning point* of World War II. With that amazing victory the world knew the Allies had won the war. It was only a matter of time before Hitler and his armies were defeated completely. But there were still many battles to be fought before he surrendered and the war was finally over.

This is a perfect analogy for the ultimate spiritual war between God and our enemy, Satan. Jesus won the victory at Calvary, defeating sin and death, and sealing the enemy's fate for eternity. But as God's children, we will continue to fight battles for His kingdom until Jesus returns. We are fighting for our lives, our families, our joy and our peace. We are also fighting to bring our loved ones, our friends and even our enemies into the family of God before it's too late. Satan knows Jesus has won, but his mission for now, is to keep as many people as he can from receiving God's saving grace and living victorious, joy-filled lives.

God has given us our battle orders. Jesus said, "Go, make disciples of all nations." (Matthew 28:19) As long as we're on this earth and Jesus has not returned, we will continue to be part of God's army, *fighting the good fight* (1 Timothy 6:12) and winning people to Christ. It's the ultimate war, the ultimate assignment, the ultimate purpose, and we are on the side of ultimate victory!

Because of God's amazing love and mercy, we stand in *His* victory as *His* children, with all the power, protection and privilege of God's royal family. We were not born into our position of royalty. We were born into sin. We have not earned our family rights. It is only because of what Christ did for us at Calvary that we can be called children of God. "How great is the love the Father has lavished on us, that we should be called children of God! And that is what we are!" (1 John 3:1)

That one act of complete and total sacrificial love not only took the punishment for our sin, but also brought us into God's family, made us children of the King of Kings, and broke the chains of sin that once bound us to the enemy's rule and power. Satan no longer has any hold on a child of God. The sin that once made him our master is gone – removed and forgotten forever. "For I will forgive their wickedness and will remember their sins no more." (Hebrews 8:12) When Christ died for mankind, He broke the enemy's power over anyone who calls Jesus Lord. As God's forgiven children we are no longer dressed in the rags of a sin-stained pauper, but in the royal white robes of Christ's righteousness. We are children of the King, set apart for Christ, to live and work and exist for His glory and His purpose.

Now that the chains of our sin are forever broken, Satan tries to defeat us with lies. He knows we belong to the King. He knows his power over us is gone, so he tries to deceive us into thinking we are not *really* God's children. His lies can never take away our inheritance, they can never remove us from God's family, but they can make us choose to give up the privilege and power that should be ours. Let me say that again… Satan's lies can *never* take away our inheritance or remove us from

God's family, but they *can* make us choose to give up the privilege and power that should be ours!

In the classic 1953 movie, *Roman Holiday* with Audrey Hepburn and Gregory Peck, Audrey plays a princess who was convinced that living the life of a commoner would be far more desirable than all the pressures and responsibilities of her royal position. When the princess runs away to see how the rest of the world lives, she meets a charming reporter played by Gregory Peck, and their exciting adventure begins.

In one early scene, the reporter finds the princess asleep on the edge of a fountain in a public square. As she wakes up and they begin talking the princess says, "You may sit down." That's a funny thing to hear coming from a woman sleeping all alone in the public square in the middle of the night, isn't it? But "You may sit down" is exactly what this princess would have said to people in her palace court, and she could not change who she was. Yes, she had taken a holiday from everything she thought was intolerable about her privileged life, but she was nonetheless, still royalty – a princess.

That movie scene paints a vivid portrait of our lives as believers. We have a new identity in Christ. You and I are royalty, and even though the enemy would like to lure us away from our Father with what he disguises as the *adventures* of commoners, we will never be anything less than children of the King. And just as the princess learned on her *Roman Holiday*, although our royal position brings with it much responsibility and yes, even battles, in the end it is the reason we have the freedom, power and honor to defend and proclaim the King's message and His kingdom to the world. We stand in the authority of our Father, the King. We represent Him. We are empowered by Him. We are protected by Him. We are loved and upheld by Him. In this war that is raging over the hearts and souls of every human being on earth, our Father's victory is our victory.

With that in mind, before we arm ourselves with a deeper understanding of our enemy's tactics, let's make sure we fully comprehend what God has promised to us as His children. God's Word not only shows us how to fight against Satan's schemes, it also tells us exactly where we stand in Jesus, because the secret to our victory is there – in Christ.

Who Are We in Christ?

We are chosen by God. God knew us and had a plan for each of our lives before we ever existed. We are adopted children, chosen specially to be part of God's family. It is an honor to be born into a royal family. But how much more incredible it is to picture God coming to the orphanage of this world, putting His hand on *your* shoulder and saying, "I want *this* child."

> For he chose us in him before the creation of
> the world to be holy and blameless in his sight.
> (Ephesians 1:4)

You may be asking yourself, "But doesn't God want everybody?" The answer is, yes! God sent His Son to die for *all* mankind. He offers His free gift of Salvation to everyone, but not everyone says yes. That is why, in his second letter to the early Christian church, Peter says this: "The Lord isn't really being slow about his promise, as some people think. No, he is being patient for your sake. He does not want *anyone* to be destroyed, but wants *everyone* to repent." (2 Peter 3:9 NLT – emphasis mine)

We are redeemed by His blood. Our sins are forgiven – *all* of them – past, present and future. When Jesus died on the cross to forgive your sins, how many of them were in the future? That's right, all of them. If all our sin was ahead of us when Jesus paid the ultimate price for our pardon, we can do nothing that He has not already forgiven. Our sins have been removed, "as far as the east is from the west." (Psalm 103:12) We have been redeemed, saved, made clean in Christ.

> In him we have redemption through his blood,
> the forgiveness of sins, in accordance with the
> riches of God's grace. (Ephesians 1:7)

We are justified by our faith in Christ. A man is said to be justified in the sight of God when in the judgment of God he is deemed righteous.[6] What a gift! God sees us as righteous, blameless, innocent, not because we *are* blameless or because we have conquered our own sin, but solely because of our faith in Christ. When God sees us, he sees His perfect Son. The enemy tries to condemn us, but his lie is quickly exposed when we know we are clothed in Christ's own righteousness. It is God who conquers our sin, and it is God who gives us what we need to conquer Satan.

> So we, too, have put our faith in Christ Jesus that we may be justified by faith in Christ and not by observing the law, because by observing the law no one will be justified. (Galatians 2:16)

We are loved unconditionally. Nothing we can ever do could make God love us less or more. His love never changes, no matter what we do or don't do. Remember, Christ died for us while we were still sinners. "But God demonstrates his own love for us in this: While we were still sinners, Christ died for us." (Romans 5:8) He doesn't say, "Get cleaned up. Stop sinning and then I'll love you." No. His love is unconditional, eternal, immeasurable, infinite, outrageous and totally amazing!

But because of his great love for us, God, who is rich in mercy, made us alive with Christ even when we were dead in transgressions … For it is by grace you have been saved, through faith – and this is not from yourselves, it is the gift of God – not by works, so that no one can boast. (Ephesians 2:4–9)

We are marked with a seal. What does that mean? What is a *seal* used for? In law, a seal is placed on an official document to attest to, or confirm that an agreement is binding and irrevocable. Our seal is the Holy Spirit, who is given to us when we accept Christ's gift of salvation, to attest to our adoption as children of God. The Spirit dwells within us and remains in us permanently, like a seal on a contract, assuring our position in God's family forever. Amazing! God Himself, the third Person of the Trinity, lives inside of mere men and women. When we say yes to the free gift of salvation, we become a dwelling place for the Creator Himself. No wonder God's Word tells us to honor God with our bodies, as *temples* of the Holy Spirit. (1 Corinthians 6:19)

And you also were included in Christ when you heard the message of truth, the gospel of your salvation. When you believed, you were marked in him with a seal, the promised Holy Spirit. (Ephesians 1:13)

We have access to God's power. As God's children, His power is available to every one of us. Much as a family of royalty or influence here on earth provides protection, power and authority to all the family members, the King of Kings provides protection, power and authority to His family as well. Most of us haven't even scratched the surface of experiencing the *incomparably great power* (Ephesians 1:19) that is available to us as God's own dearly loved children. The more intimately we *abide* in Christ, the more we are able to live in and experience the fullness of *His* power.

> I pray that the eyes of your heart may be enlightened in order that you may know the hope to which he has called you, the riches of his glorious inheritance in his holy people, and his incomparably great power for us who believe. (Ephesians 1:18–19)

We are heirs of God's kingdom with Christ. Many of us dream of inheriting millions of dollars. But as heirs of God's kingdom, He has promised us so much more than earthly riches. An heir is one who inherits what a father or another family member leaves to him. God has chosen to make His children co-heirs with Jesus, leaving to us all the promises and treasures of His kingdom. And the blessings of His kingdom are available to us now, in *this* life, as well as in the next.

> Now if we are children, then we are heirs – heirs
> of God and co-heirs with Christ, if indeed we
> share in his sufferings in order that we may also
> share in his glory. (Romans 8:17)

We are near to God. When I was growing up, my family belonged to a very legalistic church. God seemed utterly distant and unreachable to me. I learned only the dos and don'ts – how a *good girl* should act in order to please God. Religion was compartmentalized and relegated to Sunday mornings, Christmas and Easter. But God didn't fit into the reality of my everyday life. It was only when I learned of God's amazing grace, and His complete and total love for me, that I began to draw near to Him. And just as the Bible promises, when I drew near to God, He drew near to me. (James 4:8) When we can't feel Him near, it may be a good idea to ask ourselves, "Who moved?"

> But now in Christ Jesus you who once were far
> away have been brought near by the blood of
> Christ. (Ephesians 2:13)

When we stand in Christ, we have authority to stand against our enemy. God's Word calls us not so much to fight the devil, but to *resist* him. "Submit yourselves, then, to God. Resist the devil, and he will flee from you." (James 4:7) The word resist as it is used here means to "withstand." It is a term of defense rather than attack. We can stand firm and withstand Satan's schemes when we depend wholly on Christ and stand in His power, His authority and His truth, not our own.

> Therefore put on the full armor of God, so that when the day of evil comes, you may be able to stand your ground, and after you have done everything, to stand. (Ephesians 6:13)

We are God's workmanship. God is making each of us into the men and women He wants us to be. The work of the Holy Spirit in us, called *sanctification,* makes us more and more like Jesus. The enemy tries to tell us we will never be good enough to please God but the truth is, in Christ, we are already made perfect. And God's Spirit is at work in us every day, doing His sanctifying work, changing us from the inside out.

> But we ought always to thank God for you, brothers and sisters loved by the Lord, because God chose you as firstfruits to be saved through the sanctifying work of the Spirit and through belief in the truth. (2 Thessalonians 2:13)

When we think about all the promises God has made to us as His children, how could we possibly feel anything but valuable, loved, and forgiven, and stand in awe of the God who loves us? What an amazing blessing it is to know exactly where we stand in Christ; to know we are loved beyond all comprehension and completely forgiven in Him. This truth will set us free. This truth will fight the lies of Satan himself. We must know this truth so well that it will fill us with an overflowing joy that can never be taken away. In this truth, we are able to stand against all the enemy's schemes. Jesus said, "I am the way and the truth and the life." (John 14:6) Stand in truth. Stand in Jesus.

The Enemy's Schemes

Now that we understand more fully the power and privilege of our position in Christ, let's look a bit more closely at Satan's methods so we can stand with confidence, knowing how our enemy works, and how God's truth will prevail at every turn. What does the Bible tell us about Satan's strategies? As we learned in our first chapter, the enemy employs countless methods in his attempt to pull us away from our loving God and impede our effectiveness as believers. Ephesians 6:11 warns us to "Put on the full armor of God, so that you can take your stand against the devil's schemes." The word *schemes* in this passage, comes from the Greek word *methodeia*, which means scheming or craftiness. Oh yes, our enemy is crafty. He often lies and accuses us in such subtle ways we don't even know we're being tempted to doubt God.

Satan Is a Deceiver

One of Satan's most effective tactics is deceit. As a matter of fact, the very first time we hear of our enemy in Scripture is in chapter three of the book of Genesis where he, in the form of a serpent, deceives Eve in the Garden of Eden with the lie of all lies. Let's look at what happened and what *methodeia* the enemy used in his first encounter with the human race.

> Now the serpent was more crafty than any of the wild animals the LORD God had made. He said to the woman, "Did God really say, 'You must not eat from any tree in the garden'?" The woman said to the serpent, "We may eat fruit from the trees in the garden, but God did say, 'You must not eat fruit from the tree that is in the middle of the garden, and you must not touch it, or you will die.'" "You will not certainly die," the serpent said to the woman. "For God knows that when you eat from it your eyes will be opened, and you will be like God, knowing good and evil." (Genesis 3:1–5)

What exactly did Satan do here? First, he created uncertainty in Eve's mind about what God said and what His intentions were. Notice how the enemy twisted God's words. God had told Adam "You are free to eat from any tree in the garden; but you must not eat from the tree of the knowledge of good and evil, for when you eat from it you will certainly die." (Genesis 2:16-17) But what does Satan do? He creates confusion by declaring that God told them not to eat of *any* tree. He instigates trouble by suggesting God is stingy and restrictive instead of giving and kind. He says in effect, "Do you mean to tell me God expects you not to eat from *any* of the trees in this beautiful place?"

Eve was wise enough to tell the serpent that God only forbade them to eat from *one* tree. But Satan now has Eve engaged in a conversation. She says God instructed her and her husband, Adam, not to *touch* the tree or they would die. Not true. Eve is now in a very dangerous place – a debate with the great deceiver!

And Satan continued to deceive. He even called God a liar. "'You will not certainly die' the serpent said to the woman. 'For God knows that when you eat from it your eyes will be opened, and you will be like God, knowing good and evil.'" (Genesis 3:4-5)

There he goes again, twisting the truth and coloring it with lies. The fact is, when Adam and Eve ate of the tree of knowledge their eyes were opened to know good and evil. For the first time in their entire existence, they knew what it was like to disobey God. For the first time since He had breathed life into them, they felt separated from God. Do you remember what they did after they both ate from the tree? They *hid* from God. That is exactly what the enemy wanted – separation. No longer was there an unbroken, perfect relationship between God and man. By eating of the tree of the knowledge of good and evil, not only did Adam and Eve know evil, but they actually *experienced* it within themselves.

The end result of this little conversation with Satan, the ultimate deceiver, was sin, separation, death, and the beginning of Satan's reign on earth. We need to be fully aware that our enemy's tactics have not changed. To this day he is a deceiver above all things.

Satan Is an Accuser

God's Word tells us more about our adversary that can help us understand his schemes, fight back with strength, and hold on to our joy in the battle. In the book of Revelation, Satan is referred to as *the accuser of the brethren*. (Revelation 12:10) The prophet Zechariah, in a vision from God said, "Then he showed me Joshua the high priest standing before the angel of the Lord, and Satan standing at his right side to accuse him." (Zechariah 3:1) Easton's Bible Dictionary says "Satan seeks to uphold his influence among men by bringing false charges against Christians, with the view of weakening their influence and injuring the cause with which they are identified."[7]

Weaken our influence and injure our cause – that is exactly what the enemy attempts to do to every Christ follower.

Remember, Satan knows we are God's children forever. But, if he can weaken our influence with non-believers, he may prevent us from introducing others to Christ. And if he injures our cause, which is to make disciples in all nations and glorify Christ in all we do, perhaps he will prevent a few more people from experiencing the victory and joy of the kingdom of light.

How does the enemy accuse us today? Not only does he continue to accuse us before God saying, "Look what this one did," but he is also the master of whispering accusing lies to us about ourselves. How many times do you hear a voice deep in your mind saying something like this: "How could you possibly think God is going to forgive you for that? You are such a failure. You don't really think God wants to use someone like you, do you?" That is the voice of the accuser. He brings up our imperfections. He reminds us of past mistakes and paints vivid images of our sin. He pelts us with lies, half-truths and twisted logic to make us believe we are as bad, or as weak, or as much of a failure as he says we are. His accusations make us think God could never forgive us, so we give up on our faith. He makes us feel unworthy to be used by God, so we stop trying to live out our faith. His indictments make us feel guilty, so we want to hide not only from God, but also from our brothers and sisters in Christ as well. If Satan can't cause us to reject God totally, the next best thing is to make us believe his accusations, isolate us from our fellow believers, and draw us away from our loving Father who is still right here, as madly and passionately in love with us as ever.

Standing Firm

We could dive deep into many more of our enemy's schemes, strategies, and tactics, but you now have a good picture of his character and schemes. He is a liar. He deceives. He twists the truth. He accuses. He isolates. He uses anything and everything he can to destroy us and separate us from God. But God has given us everything we need to stand firm against the enemy and to continue to live in the joy and victory of Christ.

In the remaining chapters we will discover how to dress for battle, putting on the armor God has provided in order to win against Satan's schemes and attacks. Our battle plan is clearly defined in the sixth chapter of the book of Ephesians, where we are told to *put on the armor of God* and stand firm against the powers of darkness. In Christ, we can take our stand and remain standing, no matter how hard Satan tries to take us down. This is how we put on the armor of God:

- ❖ Know the truth.
  Fight the lies of the enemy with the truth of God.
- ❖ Wear Christ's robe of righteousness.
  Know your position in Christ.

❖ Walk in the peace of the gospel.
   Jesus Christ defeated sin once and for all.

❖ Hold firm to your faith.
   Let doubt push you into God's Word

❖ Be assured of your salvation.
   The price has been paid; you are forgiven, forever.

❖ Be ready to fight with God's Word.
   Fight as Jesus did – with the truth of Scripture.

❖ Pray without ceasing.
   Pray on all occasions with all kinds of prayers.

Standing in Christ – Reflections

Key Takeaway

When we ask God to take control of our minds and we choose to speak *and think* only the truth, the enemy's lies no longer have any power. Satan is defeated; his power over us was broken at the cross of Christ.

Memory Verse:

"How great is the love the Father has lavished on us, that we should be called children of God!"

(1 John 3:1)

Notes:

Standing in Christ – Study Questions

1. What lies does the enemy tell you? How does he twist the truth in your life? How do you fight back?

2. Read Romans 3:20–24 and Romans 4:4–8. Satan often tells us our sin is too bad for God to forgive. Do you ever hear that lie? What do the promises made in these two passages do to the power of that lie?

3. When Christ died, Satan thought he had won. He didn't know Christ's death and resurrection would pay our debt for sin and give us victory. Read Ephesians 2:4–10 and Colossians 3:1–4. What do these verses say about where you stand in Christ? How does being "raised with Christ" give you victory in your daily battles?

4. Read Galatians 3:26–27. How do these verses relate to God's armor (Eph. 6:10–18)? How do you clothe yourself in Christ? How does being "clothed in Christ" protect you from the enemy's schemes?

5. Read 2 Corinthians 10:3–5. How do you "take every thought captive to Christ?"

6. What is one way that putting on God's armor can help you find and keep joy in your life?

3

The Belt of Truth

Stand firm then with the belt of truth
buckled around your waist ...
Ephesians 6:14

Our Armor for Battle

Now that we have prepared our hearts and minds for
battle by remembering our true identity in Christ and
uncovering the tactics of our enemy, we're ready to dig in
and examine our battle strategy. It's time to look closely
at *God's armor*. We'll learn not only what each piece of
armor represents, but also how to put it on and keep it on
when the enemy attacks. And we will discover how each
individual article of our armor will help us hold tight to
God's gift of joy.

Approximately sixty years after the death of Jesus,
the apostle Paul wrote a letter from a Roman prison to
the Christ followers in the city of Ephesus. As he wrote,
Roman soldiers wearing the armor of the first century

guarded his prison cell. Imprisoned and unjustly accused, Paul no doubt felt the pain and turmoil of spiritual battle as he wrote to the believers in Ephesus to encourage them. Inspired by the armor worn by his captors, he warned the Ephesian church, and all believers, to put on the spiritual armor God has provided to protect us in our battles against the *spiritual forces of evil*. Paul's first instruction in arming for battle is to "Stand firm then, with the belt of truth buckled around your waist." (Ephesians 6:14) Why did Paul use the Roman soldier's belt as a metaphor for truth? Looking at the purpose of the soldier's belt will help us learn why Paul cautions us to put on our own *belt of truth*.

The Ancient Armor – The Warrior's Belt

Before a Roman soldier protected himself by putting on his battle armor, he fastened a belt, known as the *cingulum* or *balteus*, around his waist. It played a crucial role in the effectiveness of the soldier's armor, not only securing his garments, but also serving as a place on which to hang his weapons. The soldier's belt was worn at all times, even without the other

pieces of armor. Bronze plates were connected to the belt (or girdle) to protect the soldier's lower body.

God's Armor – The Belt of Truth

Just as an ancient soldier *girded* up, or secured his loins with the warrior's belt, so too we secure and protect ourselves for battle with our spiritual belt. In the book of 1 Peter God gives us this reminder, "… gird up the loins of your mind …" Our girdle, the belt upon which we hang our weapons for spiritual war, is truth. For centuries women wore girdles and other binding undergarments to tighten and hold in the not-so-firm parts of their bodies. Today both men and women buy shapewear for the same purpose. And girdle-like medical braces are often used after surgery or an abdominal injury to hold the abdomen firmly and protect the surgical site or injured area from harm. The fact is, girdles are not very comfortable but they certainly do the job. They hold us firm, control our muscles and even protect a part of our body that may be somewhat soft and weak.

Truth is like that. Truth holds us firm, keeps us under control, and protects us from the damage our enemy can inflict when we begin to get soft, believing or even beginning to live in his lies. It's interesting that Paul would use the soldier's belt or girdle to represent truth because as we mentioned above, in the first century, the warrior's belt was worn at *all* times, whether other weapons and armor were being employed or not. The same can be said of truth. No matter what kind of battle we may or may not be going through, we can never allow ourselves to be without our spiritual belt to protect us and hold us firmly in the light of God's truth.

Today, under the righteous-sounding banner of "tolerance," many would have us believe that truth is relative. They teach that what's true for you may not be true for me. Actually, this is not a new philosophy. In fact, if we go back to the time of Christ, we find Pilot asking the age-old question as Jesus stands before him, while the Jews clamor for His execution.

> "You are a king, then!" said Pilate. Jesus answered, "You are right in saying I am a king. In fact, for this reason I was born, and for this I came into the world, to testify to the truth. Everyone on the side of truth listens to me." "What is truth?" Pilate asked. With this he went out again to the Jews and said, "I find no basis for a charge against him." (John 18:37–38)

What is truth? Is there any real answer to this age-old question? Absolutely. If we search God's Word, we find that truth is anything but relative. It is firmly established in the God of creation and in His Son. Here are just a few of the 145 references in the Bible (New International Version) to help assure us of the truth about truth.

❖ Sanctify them by the truth; your word is truth. (John 17:17)

❖ Jesus answered, "I am the way and the truth and the life …" (John 14:6)

❖ Then you will know the truth, and the truth will set you free. (John 8:32)

❖ … no lie comes from the truth. (1 John 2:21)

❖ But when he, the Spirit of truth comes, he will guide you into all truth. (John 16:13)

Do not be fooled. Truth exists and it is the same for everyone. We don't live in a world of gray-tones and relative reality where the truth for you is different from the truth for me. God's Word is truth. We can stake our lives on it. But to fight against the lies of Satan, we have to *know* the truth. Understanding that God has given us definitive truth is not enough. Our enemy, the devil, twists the truth, attempting to manipulate our minds so we believe anything and everything *except* the truth. But Jesus told us that when we know the truth, it will set us free. (John 8:32) The truth will destroy the enemy's lies, trickery and deception. Gird yourself in truth. Bind it around your waist at all times, in the heat of battle and in the peace of the valley. Hang your sword on the belt of truth, and fight this battle to win!

Satan's Schemes Against Truth

Satan is a liar. In John 8:44 Jesus, speaking of Satan, said, "When he lies, he speaks his native language, for he is a liar and the father of lies." In our last chapter we talked about the enemy's tactics and schemes. Let's take a closer look now at how Satan tries to destroy us by attacking the truth.

As we have said, one of the enemy's most active and effective battlegrounds is our mind. That is where we fight the battle for truth. What we choose to believe, focus on and put into our minds will either protect and defend us, or become tools the enemy uses to pull us away from God. When we saturate our minds in truth, Satan's goal of deception is much more difficult to achieve. But when we don't put a guard at the door of our minds, the devil can begin to turn our thoughts away from truth, and from God. How does he do that? What gets us confused or makes us focus on the wrong things?

Although Satan is not omniscient (all knowing) or omnipresent (everywhere at once), we must never make the mistake of thinking he is not powerful. He does not have the ability to know your thoughts, but based on your words and actions he has all the clues he needs to figure you out. And he does have the ability to speak lies into your mind. As a child of God, when you find yourself thinking negative, destructive or just plain sinful thoughts, remember, those kinds of ideas surely don't come from your new identity in Christ. They come from your old sin nature, which is the human side of you that still listens to the god of this world, Satan.

When we became followers of Christ, we were filled with the Holy Spirit, but the Spirit's work in us is not finished yet. It won't be complete until we are fully sanctified and made like Christ in the next life. While we are here on earth, a battle goes on within us. Our old sin nature constantly fights against our new nature in Christ. (Galatians 5:17) Satan will go to extraordinary lengths to defeat us by making our old sin nature the victor.

In this war that takes place on the battlefield of our mind, it is vitally important to *take our thoughts captive to Christ* (2 Corinthians 10:5). That is not an easy concept to fully understand, so perhaps it will help to imagine what it was like when Paul was taken captive by the Roman soldiers who imprisoned him. First the soldiers had to find and capture Paul. Next they would have restrained him in some way to prevent his escape. And finally, he would have been escorted and handed over to the governor or other Roman official to determine his fate.

Taking our thoughts captive to Christ follows the same pattern. First, we *find and capture* every thought that goes through our mind, asking the Holy Spirit to help us discern between truth and lies. Next we *restrain* the lies, by not giving them free reign in our minds. And finally we *hand over* the lies to Christ, our King.

We can't always stop the thoughts the enemy puts in our minds, but we can choose to reject the lies as soon as we recognize them. By taking our thoughts captive to Christ, we choose what we allow to *remain* in our minds. When we permit Satan's lies to take root and don't fight back by rejecting them with the strength, power and truth of God's Word, they settle in and take up residency. This was the mistake Eve made. She let the lies in and engaged Satan in a conversation. Once the enemy gains a foothold, the lies that were previously just bothersome visitors, become self-invited strongholds.

When we play with the thoughts and deceptions of the enemy and don't immediately take them captive, giving them to Christ, they make themselves at home because in reality, we have welcomed them in. When we allow a lie or evil thought to take up residency, it is much more difficult to drive it out than if we had given it to Christ the moment it first entered our mind. Ephesians 4:27 tells us not to give the devil a foothold. We must fill our minds with truth. We must speak the truth. We must live in the truth.

By now, if you are anything like me, you are probably asking: "What would it look like in *my* life to live in the truth and take my thoughts captive to Christ?" Perhaps a real-life example will help. I've changed the names but this story is true.

After going back to school in his early forties, Sam's ambition to start a new mid-life career became a reality when he was hired to do his "dream job." Sam learned very quickly though, that doing a job in the corporate world looks nothing like what he had experienced in the classroom. He was more than a bit intimidated as he took his place in the new company. Sam's boss had every confidence in his abilities, and as the months passed Sam was learning and doing more than he had ever dreamed possible. Things were going beautifully until one of his coworkers decided Sam was not really qualified for his job, and went on a mission to make his life miserable, or worse, to destroy Sam's reputation and his career.

With the coworker's constant attacks day after day, all of Sam's old insecurities came back and his mind was filled with questions and lies. "You're just not smart enough to do this job." "Maybe he's right. Maybe you are a faker." "What would ever make you think you could succeed at this career?" "You are a failure." "You are an imposter."

Sam's redemption from the barrage of lies filling his mind, not only from his coworker but even more strongly from the Father of Lies, came by saturating his mind with truth and learning to take every thought captive to Christ. Each morning before work, Sam would spend an hour praying and reading God's Word. He wrote down, underlined, and highlighted all the biblical passages that spoke truth to counter the lies swirling around in his mind. Once armed with the truth of God's Word, Sam was able to stop himself every time one of the destructive thoughts came to mind. He would pray, "Father God, in Jesus name I ask you to take control of my mind. If there is any truth in these thoughts, or in what my coworker is saying, please show me. Help me to deal honestly with my shortcomings and give me discernment to reject any lies. Take those false thoughts Jesus, and replace them with Your truth."

Once Sam took his thoughts captive and gave them to Christ, he would continue to arm himself with truth – reading and praying all the Scripture he had found to refute and defuse the lies he heard in his mind. Sam read those verses out loud, proclaiming to the enemy that he had no power over his thoughts because he was filled with truth and with the Holy Spirit of God. The enemy's lies were defeated and lost their power over Sam.

But that's not the end of the story. During those hours and hours of prayer and digging into God's Word, Sam also heard God whispering, "Pray for your enemy." This coworker who Satan wanted to use not only to destroy Sam's dream, but also to ruin his witness as a believer in this very secular new workplace, could have pushed him to the edge and made him react to the attacks in a very ungodly way. But Sam listened to God. He prayed for his "enemy." He prayed not only the easy

"Bless his family." prayers, but also the hard "Help him succeed in his career." and "Lead him to Jesus." prayers as well. Satan's plans were defeated.

Sam was a true warrior, taking his thoughts captive to Christ and wearing the belt of truth. But remember, our enemy is crafty. Satan often makes lies sound like truth, even using Scripture which he knows better than we do. He twists the truth of God to get us ever so slightly off track, because that's all he needs to push us further and further away from God. It's a bit like veering off the path when you're hiking in the mountains. Suppose you're on a walking trail heading toward your destination, maybe a beautiful waterfall, when a noise in the bushes distracts you and takes you just a little off the marked trail. If you continue walking without correcting your course, soon you will no longer be just a little off track. You'll find yourself deep in the woods with no clue how to get back to the comfort of the well-worn trail. It's that way with listening to the enemy's lies. The longer we keep walking down the path of untruth that in the beginning seemed just slightly off base, the farther away we wander and our destination becomes harder and harder to find.

Let me give you a real example from my own life. Years ago I was introduced to a very "hip" television show that was not only interesting and funny, but very well done; with excellent acting as well as exceptional writing and storylines. I became more than a fan. I was addicted. There was just one problem. Like so many others, this TV show came from a very secular point of view, and soon I regarded the things I heard and saw there as simply "real life." I accepted language and storylines that were far from godly. I reasoned that as an adult, I could enjoy the good parts of the show and reject the bad.

But I had gotten off course. I was beginning to accept other questionable ideas, considering them "normal." The enemy did not have to pull me all the way into something blatantly evil like pornography. He took me just a little off of the biblical standard and soon my thoughts, my decisions, and even my language were not what God would choose for me. The moral of the story is this: Stay on the course of truth! Don't let yourself get even a *tiny* bit off track or before you know it, you won't be able to recognize the enemy's lies when you hear them.

Finally, watch out for the seeds of doubt Satan plants along his path of deception as well. He will often enhance his original lie with confusion, trying to get us to question what we know is true. As we find ourselves believing Satan's lies and fighting to get back to the solid path of truth, he comes along with yet another set of lies, this time telling us how wrong we were to believe the truth in the first place. Our best defense is to know the truth so well, we can recognize a lie the minute we hear it.

Putting On the Belt of Truth

So, how do we squeeze into this new girdle of ours to give our minds a firm foundation in truth? I believe God's Word provides us with three important principles that will enable us to put on the belt of truth.

Know the truth. Memorize Scripture so you can fight the enemy's lies just as Jesus did. It is critical to be able to call God's Word to mind when we are in the midst of temptation or fighting against Satan's lies. But knowing the truth is more than simply being able to quote Scripture. We must also know the principles of God's Word. We need to understand biblical truth about everything in life, because the enemy will use our lack of understanding to deceive us. Although false teachers speak convincingly and with authority, they teach lies.

> For the time will come when men will not put up with sound doctrine. Instead, to suit their own desires, they will gather around them a great number of teachers to say what their itching ears want to hear. (2 Timothy 4:3)

We need to be knowledgeable of the truth, using godly discernment to recognize a lie when we hear it. That kind of shrewdness only comes as we become a student of God's Word. Matthew 10:15 says "I am sending you out like sheep among wolves. Therefore be as shrewd as snakes and as innocent as doves." Spend time in the Word. Don't just read the Bible, study it.

> Jesus said, "If you hold to my teaching, you are really my disciples. Then you will know the truth, and the truth will set you free."
> (John 8:31–32)

Live in the truth. It's not enough just to know the truth. If we don't live according to the truth, we are like people who know they are sick, know how to get well, and yet continue to live in a way that leads to death. Think about that. If you had a life-threatening disease and the doctor told you exactly what to do to get well, would you ignore him and let yourself die? Unfortunately, many people do just that. They keep smoking after a lung cancer diagnosis, or keep drinking when they already have liver damage, or don't take the medication they need regularly for life-threatening diabetes.

We can do the same with the truth of God. We can memorize Scripture, read the Word, go to church and do Bible studies, but still choose to live in the lies the enemy tells us or that we choose to tell ourselves. If we are going to wear the belt of truth and fight the deception and lies of the enemy, it's not enough to just know the truth and recognize the lies. We must choose to *live in the truth* every day.

What does living in the truth look like? It is acting on what we know is true. It is doing what we know is right, no matter how hard it is or how much the enemy tries to convince us it will end in disaster. It is being willing to obey God's *still small voice* (1 Kings 19:12) even when we are afraid or don't know what the outcome will be. Living in the truth is acting upon what we know is God's truth no matter what, and trusting our loving Father for the results.

> Teach me your way, O LORD, and I will walk in your truth; give me an undivided heart, that I may fear your name. (Psalm 86:11)

Speak the truth. Choose to be bold and declare the truth. Speak it unashamedly. Theologian H. H. Hobbs said this about declaring truth, "People often speak of defending truth. That's well and good, but truth is not so weak that it cannot defend itself. What is needed most is to declare the truth in love. If let loose in the arena of ideas truth will defend itself. Truth is of God – falsehood is of Satan."[8]

Don't let the enemy's deceptions take hold in your mind or on your lips. Speak what you know is true, even when you are in the midst of a battle with doubt. Our minds respond to spoken words, and so do our hearts. Speak the truth and experience the power of hearing and responding to it. Then watch the enemy flee when the lies he puts in your mind are broken, as you take every thought captive to Christ and speak truth boldly and clearly for both the spiritual and physical world to hear.

> "These are the things you are to do: Speak the truth to each other, and render true and sound judgment in your courts; do not plot evil against your neighbor, and do not love to swear falsely. I hate all this," declares the LORD.
> (Zechariah 8:16–17)

In many ways, Satan has succeeded in silencing the truth in society today. Political correctness and fear of retribution or bullying has silenced many believers. Christians must be respectful but never silent when confronted with Satan's lies.

JAN'S BATTLE: FIGHTING BACK WITH TRUTH

When I feel hurt, I naturally tend to beat myself up, harshly judge the other person, distance myself, or all the above. My mind battles to not sink into shame, to forgive, to pray for the offender, to confront in love, and to guard against bitterness. Each of these battles takes consciously thinking of many of God's truths.

For example, to fight shame I focus on verses expressing God's extravagant love for me. I am the apple of His eye. He never leaves me or forsakes me. He tenderly collects my tears in a bottle. He uses trials to discipline me because He loves me; He promises to shape me into the image of Christ. My favorite battle verse to fight shame is Psalm 34:4–5.

To keep from harshly judging the person who hurt me, I ask Jesus to take my mind captive. Usually, I don't think to do this until it's too late. It's such a knee-jerk reaction to name-call or to assume the person had a hurtful motive. Then, when I recognize I'm angry because I think the person is hard-hearted, selfish, or obviously doesn't care about me, I confess those judgments and ask God to help me forgive my offender. Often the Holy Spirit will take the log out of my eye by showing me how I have done the same thing to others. Jesus said, "Do not judge, or you too will be judged." I'm still trying to develop a habit of obeying this command right away. It's still a battle for me.

When I find I'm avoiding people who have hurt me, my battle verses become the ones about not letting a "bitter root grow up" and about "guarding my heart." I almost always have to ask God to help me walk the fine line between those two so that my responses are healthy and love-motivated. When the evil one tempts me to think I'm better than my offender, I fight with verses warning about pride. When someone puts me down, I tend to quickly judge: Oh, they just can't feel good about themselves unless they condescend to others. If I hang on to that judgment instead of confessing it, the Holy Spirit shines His light on my heart and reminds me that I am building myself up by thinking poorly of others. That's basically what bitterness is. I battle bitterness with verses about God's being close to the brokenhearted, protecting the weak and avenging wrongs. As Psalm 144:1 says, God is faithful in training my hands for war.

Freedom and Joy in Truth

We have learned much about our belt of truth, the first piece of spiritual armor God provides for his children. But how does girding ourselves in truth bring us joy? What do truth and joy have to do with each other? I believe the answer to that question lies in the freedom we find in truth. God's Word promises that the truth will set us free. (John 8:31) But there is more. Jesus didn't stop there as He spoke to the Jewish believers about truth.

> To the Jews who had believed him, Jesus said, "If you hold to my teaching, you are really my disciples. Then you will know the truth, and the truth will set you free." They answered him, "We are Abraham's descendants and have never been slaves of anyone. How can you say that we shall be set free?" Jesus replied, "I tell you the truth, everyone who sins is a slave to sin. Now a slave has no permanent place in the family, but a son belongs to it forever. So if the Son sets you free, you will be free indeed." (John 8:31–36)

We are freed from our slavery to sin because the Son Himself has set us free. And our freedom from sin has been sealed by God's Holy Spirit living inside us, "… and where the Spirit of the Lord is, there is freedom." (2 Corinthians 3:17) It is in the miracle of God's Spirit living in us that we find our guarantee of freedom. It is in the truth of our freedom from sin that we are filled with hope, peace and joy. We are no longer bound by the chains in which the enemy's lies would entangle us. In Christ, filled with His Spirit, we have the freedom to live without fear, without guilt, and without the bondage to the sin that once held us as slaves to darkness. In the light of truth, we can know and trust our gracious, merciful Savior to set us free indeed. Now that's true joy!

Today, as you memorize the Scripture verse and dig deep to ponder the study questions about truth at the end of this chapter, ask God to open your mind and your heart, and to fill you with the freedom and joy that come from living in the truth. Ask Him to show you where you may be listening to and believing the lies of the enemy. Remember, Satan's lies are often sneaky. They can disguise themselves in very convincing theology and spiritual language, or be introduced in everyday activities like watching TV or searching the Internet. Pray that God would open your eyes, give you discernment, and reveal where you may need to tighten your belt of truth.

The Belt of Truth – Reflections

Key Takeaway:

When we allow Satan's lies to take root in our minds and don't fight back by rejecting them with the strength, power and truth of God, the lies settle in and take up residency.

Memory Verse:

"If you hold to my teaching, you are really my disciples. Then you will know the truth, and the truth will set you free." (John 8:31)

Notes:

The Belt of Truth – Study Questions

1. Read John 16:12–14. Do you believe there is definitive truth? How do you answer someone who says, "What's true for you might not be true for me"?

2. In John 8:31-32 Jesus said, "If you hold to my teaching, you are really my disciples. Then you will know the truth, and the truth will set you free." How does the truth set you free?

3. Read 2 Corinthians 11:2–4. Has your "mind been led astray from your sincere and pure devotion to Christ?" How does the enemy deceive you and lead you astray?

4. 2 John 1:4 says, "It has given me great joy to find some of your children walking in the truth, just as the Father commanded us." What does walking in the truth (or living in the truth) look like in your life? Is it hard?

5. Read Ephesians 4:14–16. Why it is important not only to believe the truth, but to speak the truth as well? How does speaking the truth defeat Satan's schemes and lies?

6. Read Romans 8:1–3. How does knowing the truth of your freedom in Christ bring you joy?

4

The Breastplate of Righteousness

He put on righteousness as his breastplate,
and the helmet of salvation on his head
Isaiah 59:17

A Righteousness Not Our Own

How does it feel to be dressing for battle? The adversary
we face as a soldier in God's army is fierce, but with
God's belt of truth buckled around our waists, we are
beginning to arm ourselves for victory. Our foundation is
solid. No matter what schemes the enemy uses against us,
we are girded in truth. We are held secure in the
knowledge of the truth of God's Word. We can take
every thought captive to Christ and stand firm no matter
what kind of deception the enemy is hurling at us.

But be alert. The Bible tells us that in this battle
against the powers, principalities and the kingdom of
darkness, we will need to put on more than just a belt.
Our battle orders from the apostle Paul in Ephesians 6

tell us the next piece of armor we are to put on is the *breastplate of righteousness*. Our breastplate provides an additional layer of defense and protection when the enemy launches his inevitable attacks.

> Stand firm then, with the belt of truth buckled around your waist, with the breastplate of righteousness in place ... (Ephesians 6:14)

Let's begin as we did in our last chapter, by learning a bit more about what Paul saw the Roman soldiers wearing as he sat in prison and wrote to the church at Ephesus. Then we'll look at how and why Paul compared that Roman breastplate to our unparalleled gift of the righteousness of Christ.

The Ancient Armor – The Metal Breastplate

The breastplate of a Roman soldier was a coat or tunic comprised of one or more pieces of bronze, iron or chain. The iron or bronze armor was built in four sections, covering the shoulders, chest and back, and protecting the heart and other vital organs. The metal plates were sewn to a stiff leather vest, which was

put on like a jacket before the front plates were tied with leather straps.

God's Armor – The Breastplate of Righteousness

How interesting that Paul uses the metaphor of the warrior's breastplate to represent righteousness. The fact is, in ancient times when soldiers protected themselves with armor, wearing a breastplate was not a guarantee of safety. The metal breastplate was far from impregnable. In 1 Kings 22:34 we see that the king of Israel is wounded right through his breastplate.

> But someone drew his bow at random and hit the king of Israel between the sections of his armor. The king told his chariot driver, "Wheel around and get me out of the fighting. I've been wounded." (1 Kings 22:34)

And in the book of 1 Samuel, Saul is critically wounded in spite of being dressed, undoubtedly, in his full battle armor.

> The fighting grew fierce around Saul, and when the archers overtook him, they wounded him critically. (1 Samuel 31:3)

Our breastplate would also be vulnerable to the piercing arrows being hurled at us from our very able enemy if this vital piece of protective mesh was woven from *our own* righteousness. How many holes are in that? But thank God, in His mercy, grace, and wisdom, He has made our breastplate from the solid, impenetrable, unshakable righteousness of Jesus Christ Himself. If our defense depended upon our own righteousness, who could stand? (Psalm 130:3) God knew our weakness and limitations, so He provided a way to save us from the chains of sin and defeat. He clothed us in the righteousness of His perfect Son.

> What is more, I consider everything a loss because of the surpassing worth of knowing Christ Jesus my Lord, for whose sake I have lost all things. I consider them garbage, that I may gain Christ and be found in him, not having a righteousness of my own that comes from the law, but that which is through faith in Christ – the righteousness that comes from God on the basis of faith. (Philippians 3:8-9)

When we wear Christ's righteousness instead of our own, we are protected by a breastplate Satan's arrows cannot penetrate. Yet he continues to hurl his flaming darts relentlessly, hoping to find a break in our armor.

Our enemy does not aim first at the shoulder or the arm, but rather at the heart. It is here that the poison on the tip of his arrow penetrates and turns the heart from love to hate, generosity to selfishness and kindness to brutality. And it is here, in the heart, that his accusations of unrighteousness then turn our hearts away from God to the guilt and self-condemnation that defeat us.

Only God is truly righteous. Only He is sinless perfection. Only He is able to stand against all scrutiny and accusation and be found *not guilty*. That is why when God, in all His wisdom and perfect justice, graciously set His plan in place to free mankind from the guilt and punishment of our sin, the answer was not to make *us* holy. Our righteousness could never be enough.

All of us have become like one who is unclean,

and all our righteous acts are like filthy rags.

(Isaiah 64:6)

God's answer was to cover us in the perfect, righteous, holiness of His son. He removes our sin *as far as the east is from the west* (Psalm 103:12) and fills the empty, gaping hole with the perfection, holiness, and righteousness of His one and only Son. What a gift! What an exchange – the righteousness of our Savior in exchange for our wretched sin.

In this chapter we will look closely at the gift of Christ's righteousness and the power it gives us to fight against the lies and schemes of the enemy. We'll consider the righteousness of God, the unrighteousness of man, and how God's incredible gift has taken away our guilt and shame and broken the power of sin in our lives.

God's Righteousness

The Bible tells us we serve a righteous and holy God. But what exactly is righteousness? The Merriam-Webster Dictionary defines it as: *acting in accord with divine or moral law: free from guilt or sin.* Righteousness is true holiness, perfection, a state of being completely sinless. Who is sinless but the Creator God Himself? Who acts totally in accord with divine law except the One who is divine? The Bible says so much about God's righteousness, I hardly know where to begin. The word righteous (or righteousness) is used five hundred twenty-four times in the New International Version of the Bible. Let's look at what just a few of these passages tell us about this aspect of God's amazing character.

Righteousness is part of God's character. It is who He is, not just what He does. Everything about God is without flaw, completely holy, truly righteous. That is why it is impossible for Him to be united or intimately related to anything or anyone who is not perfectly holy. Sin is appalling to God. It is an affront to His very nature.

> Your righteousness reaches to the skies, O God,
> you who have done great things. Who, O God,
> is like you? (Psalm 71:19)

God's ways are righteous. Not only is righteousness who God is, but everything He does is also righteous. Even when we, as mere humans, don't understand or agree, God's actions, His plans and everything He allows or does not allow are perfectly righteous and just. God truly is the *only* righteous one. And since God is God and we are not, we need to trust that His ways are higher than ours and believe in His righteousness and goodness even when we don't fully understand.

> "For my thoughts are not your thoughts, neither
> are your ways my ways," declares the LORD.
> "As the heavens are higher than the earth, so are
> my ways higher than your ways and my thoughts
> than your thoughts." (Isaiah 55:8–9)

God's righteousness is everlasting. What a comforting thought, knowing that God never changes. Think about how unsettling it is when someone you love is not consistent and changes his or her mind or actions constantly. It's hard to trust someone like that, isn't it? We never quite know where we stand with that kind of person. But the truth is, God is the same yesterday, today and tomorrow. He will always be holy, perfect and righteous in all He is and all He does.

> Your righteousness is everlasting and your law is true. (Psalm 119:142)

God's laws are righteous. God's laws are not burdensome. As a matter of fact, they liberate us to live a life free from guilt, pain, heartache and sin. One of the best books I ever read on the topic was an early publication by Bill Hybels, *Laws That Liberate*. It is still available today in the form of a Bible study. The truth we need to fully understand is that God's laws are righteous, and they bring us freedom!

> You are righteous, LORD, and your laws are right. (Psalm 119:137)

God judges in righteousness. If you have ever been in court fighting for your rights in a legal battle, you know how you hope the person hearing your case is a righteous judge. God is a righteous judge. He is a God of justice. It is the very nature of His righteousness and justice that demands our sin not go unpunished. Justice requires payment for sin. (Romans 6:23) But praise God, in His mercy and grace He took the punishment due to us upon Himself. What a God we have!

Let all creation rejoice before the LORD, for he comes, he comes to judge the earth. He will judge the world in righteousness and the peoples in his faithfulness. (Psalm 96:13)

The righteousness of our awesome God is perfect, unchangeable and indisputable. God is good, all the time. When we are covered in His righteousness, we are covered completely and fully protected. None of Satan's arrows can penetrate this breastplate.

Man's Unrighteousness

The Word of God is clear – we have no righteousness of our own. (Psalm 14:1–3; Psalm 53:1–3; Ecclesiastes 7:20; Romans 3:10) "But wait!" you may say. "I'm not so bad. Look at all the good things I do. I help people. I give money to charity. I donate to the poor. I love my family. Why would the Bible say my righteousness is like filthy rags?" Because true righteousness means being completely without sin – it is the perfection of our Holy God and we all fall far short of that! All our good deeds and righteous acts are imperfect, whether in motive or substance, when compared with the ultimate flawless holiness of God. And no matter how hard we try, no matter how many good works we do, we can never make ourselves good enough, or worthy enough to be in an intimate relationship with a perfectly righteous God.

But because He loves us, God did for us what we could not do for ourselves. He created a way to *justify us* – that is, to make us righteous in His sight – as though we had never sinned. (Romans 3:21–24) Through our faith in what Christ did for us on the cross, God has given us His righteousness. The righteousness we have in Christ enables us to rest in the joy of an intimate relationship with God. The righteousness we have in Christ allows us to stand firm, freeing us from the guilt, accusations and lies of the enemy. When Satan shoots his arrows at our breastplate by telling us we can never be good enough to please God, we stand in victory because our breastplate is the impenetrable, perfect, never ceasing righteousness of our Savior.

Let's look closer now at what God's Word tells us about our own human righteousness and the righteousness of Christ that covers all who trust in Him.

We have no righteousness of our own. God's Word says so unmistakably. Christ set the bar high. We are stained by sin and can do nothing to make ourselves clean.

> For I tell you that unless your righteousness surpasses that of the Pharisees and the teachers of the law, you will certainly not enter the kingdom of heaven. (Matthew 5:20)

Righteousness is a free gift. God knew we could never meet His standard of perfect holiness. He knew we would always fall short of His glory and holiness. That is why He gave us His own righteousness as a gift. It is completely free, never earned.

> This righteousness from God comes through faith in Jesus Christ to all who believe. There is no difference, for all have sinned and fall short of the glory of God, and are justified freely by his grace through the redemption that came by Christ Jesus. (Romans 3:22–24)

Righteousness does not come from obedience. The Bible tells us that God gave us His laws to make us fully aware of our sin. (Romans 7:7) No matter how good we are, we can never keep the perfect law of God. Praise God that He has given us His righteousness apart from the law.

> Clearly no one who relies on the law is justified before God, because "the righteous will live by faith." (Galatians 3:11)

Righteousness comes by faith. We will never attain righteousness through our works. We will never be good enough to satisfy a perfect, holy God. But when we put our faith in Christ, our unrighteousness is covered by Christ's righteousness.

> This righteousness is given through faith in
> Jesus Christ to all who believe. (Romans 3:22)

Righteousness comes through Christ. Only through what Christ did for us on the cross can we stand forgiven and clothed in His righteousness. We are completely dependent on Jesus. Without His sacrifice and forgiveness we stand accused – sinful from birth.

> God made him who had no sin to be sin for us,
> so that in him we might become the righteousness of God. (2 Corinthians 5:21)

What a blessing. What amazing grace. We can have joy because of what our loving Father has done on our behalf. In spite of our desperate sin, His love provides a way for us to be united to Him forever. Never forget, as a forgiven child of God you are covered in the righteousness of Jesus Christ. Your Abba Father sees you as His perfect, sinless child, not because of what you have done, not because of your own acts of righteousness or obedience, but because of what *He* has done for you in redemption through His Son.

Satan's Schemes Against Righteousness

Although we are covered in Christ's blood and are seen by our heavenly Father as clean, justified, forgiven children, Satan will lie and twist the truth, telling us we will never be good enough. One of the enemy's most effective tools is legalism – a belief that says we must be good in order to be forgiven and loved by God.

Hmm … conditional love, now that does not sound like the God of the Bible, does it? And yet, that is what millions and millions of people are led to believe every day. If the enemy can keep us in the "be good so God will be happy with you" mindset, he now has abundant fuel to feed his accusations and lies. For who has not sinned? Who does not continue to sin and make mistakes? Even the apostle Paul fought with sin and battled to live a life that reflected Jesus. If, like the Pharisees of Jesus' day, we think we need to keep every letter of the law in order to be loved and forgiven, we are destined to fail and feel unloved by God.

> So I find this law at work: When I want to do good, evil is right there with me. For in my inner being I delight in God's law; but I see another law at work in the members of my body, waging war against the law of my mind and making me a prisoner of the law of sin at work within my members. What a wretched man I am! Who will

rescue me from this body of death? Thanks be to God – through Jesus Christ our Lord! So then, I myself in my mind am a slave to God's law, but in the sinful nature a slave to the law of sin. Therefore, there is now no condemnation for those who are in Christ Jesus, because through Christ Jesus the law of the Spirit of life set me free from the law of sin and death. (Romans 7:21–8:2)

The Bible tells us the law was given in order to make us aware of our sin. (Romans 7:7) Jesus Himself set the bar even higher than that of the Old Testament law.

You have heard that it was said to the people long ago, "Do not murder, and anyone who murders will be subject to judgment." But I tell you that anyone who is angry with his brother will be subject to judgment. Again, anyone who says to his brother, "Raca," is answerable to the Sanhedrin. But anyone who says, "You fool!" will be in danger of the fire of hell. (Matthew 5:21–22)

Why did Jesus set the bar so high? Did He really expect us to be even holier than the Pharisees who tried to keep every one of the six hundred and thirteen Old Testament laws? No! He was showing us we can't possibly be good enough to appease a holy God. He was demonstrating the futility of man's attempt to be holy, and the incredible grace and power of what He was about to do for us. Without Jesus' death and resurrection, no one can ever be justified – not by our obedience, not by our acts of righteousness, and not by our good works. Only by His one act of inexplicable sacrifice can we be made righteous – by His free gift – a gift that can never be taken away.

So, what does our enemy, the devil do? He tries to keep us locked into the pointless self-condemnation of the law. He whispers, "So you think Jesus died for you, but do you *really* think He's going to love you if you can't even stop doing that? He's not going to forgive *that* sin." The theology of *grace plus works* has been accepted and taught by many churches over the centuries of Christianity. I believe the enemy revels in Christian churches that keep people on a treadmill of good works, never fully teaching the truth of freedom and complete forgiveness in Jesus Christ. But when we know we are forgiven, clothed in the righteousness of Jesus Himself, our enemy's accusations are powerless. Then, like Jesus Himself, we can truly say, "Get thee behind me Satan" (Matthew 16:23) and know that our Father sees us as His righteous, forgiven, pure children, who have been washed in the blood of the Lamb.

But remember, Satan is extremely crafty, so he does not try to defeat us in the area of righteousness in just one way. Not only does he accuse us and tell us we're not good enough to be loved by God, he also uses righteousness in just the opposite way. He can wreak havoc with a Christian's self-righteousness just as well as with our self-condemnation. How does he do that? Think about how often you have met Christians who made you feel they were somehow just a bit *holier* than you. Oh, they never say that. But their actions, their questions, their well-meaning suggestions all scream, "If you were really a Christian, you would ..." There seems to be a kind of friendliness with just an edge of pity for the poor person who just doesn't quite know Jesus the way *we* do. The enemy loves the self-righteous hypocrisy that separates believer from believer and chases away anyone seeking Jesus faster than a swarm of bees! If Satan can't make us feel guilty, he'll settle for making us feel a bit better than others. And the result? People who need to see and feel the love of Christ are disappointed at best and devastated at worst.

Never forget that our enemy is a deceiver. He will take the truth of God's Word and twist it to throw us off base, taking us to a place that eventually won't even resemble God's awesome gift of Christ's righteousness in the slightest. Put on your breastplate! Protect your heart with the knowledge and assurance of your complete forgiveness and justification in Christ. But just as importantly, don't let the enemy deceive you into thinking your new righteousness in Christ is your own. We have no room for pride, when the truth is we are sinners, covered and clothed in the righteousness of the Almighty.

BRENDA'S STORY: SATAN'S PLAYGROUND

I have found that the battles I lose most often have to do with Christians who don't think they need forgiveness. They stomp on my heart and go their merry way. Christians often break promises and they act selfishly, leaving me to clean up the mess. They don't care to admit their addictions, they judge and blame others, and the list goes on.

That's when the enemy can easily inspire unforgiveness and bitterness in me. Satan's playground is the self-righteousness of Christians who don't see their own sin in little daily thought patterns and actions. Everyone touched by them wonders where God is. Not knowing when we, as believers, need forgiveness fosters our further sin.

Putting On the Breastplate of Righteousness

Now that we know we stand covered in the righteousness of Jesus Christ, and have looked at some of the ways the enemy twists, deceives and uses righteousness to bring people down, it's time to consider just how we put on our breastplate. The Bible has a lot to say about followers of Christ living righteous lives. If we're not careful, we can easily begin listening to the enemy telling us we'd better get our act together, or God won't love us anymore. The fact is, God's desire for us is not only to wear the righteousness of His Son, but also to *become* like Jesus. Through sanctification, the Holy Spirit living in us remakes us into the image of Christ. As we grow in our relationship with the Lord and allow the Spirit to work in our lives, we begin to change. We see the fruit of the Holy Spirit in our lives as we submit to God, saying "Yes Lord, whatever you want – I want."

So when we read passages like 1 John 3:7–9 that tell us we will not go on sinning if we are "born of God," I believe God is showing us what can and will be, as we allow *Him* to work in us. We can't make ourselves righteous. But as we make ourselves available to the Holy Spirit and obey His promptings, one day at a time, *He transforms us* into the image of Christ more and more each day. Our own righteousness will never be complete as long as we're in these physical bodies. We will always struggle with sin and fight to live according to the standards of a Holy God just as the apostle Paul did. But as we walk with our Lord day by day, each time we say yes to Him, we allow God to bring us one step closer in His lifelong process of conforming us to the likeness of Jesus. As we walk this path with the Holy Spirit, allowing Him to mold and make us into the likeness of our King, how do we put on Christ's righteousness and fight the lies of the enemy? I believe we keep our breastplate fastened tight and fight this battle to win in at least four important ways.

Cease striving. We need to remind ourselves that this work of becoming righteous is not our job – it is God's work in us. We can bask in the joy and peace of knowing we already stand faultless before God's throne of grace. When we stop trying so hard to be good, and seek instead to get close to Jesus, our lives will reflect who He has *already* made us to be. Our righteousness comes by faith, not by works. As long as we rely on God's righteousness and not our own, we have no reason for pride, and no reason for condemnation. What freedom is in that truth!

> Therefore, there is now no condemnation for those who are in Christ Jesus, because through Christ Jesus the law of the Spirit of life set me free from the law of sin and death.
> (Romans 8:1–2)

Seek Christ. Stay in God's Word, and spend time with your Savior. When we know Him, we know the truth, and He will show us the things He wants to change in us as we walk this path of life with Him. It's a process, and our transformation is God's work of love, patience and eternal grace. As you draw closer and closer to Jesus, the wonder of His forgiveness and mercy will astonish you more every day. It is in that wonder, and yes even joy, that we stand in a place where the enemy can't touch us – a place he doesn't even understand – a place of true love and complete surrender.

> Therefore, if anyone is in Christ, he is a new creation; the old has gone, the new has come! (2 Corinthians 5:17)

Act like a child of the King. Remember who you are. You are the son or daughter of the King of Kings, and you are completely forgiven in Christ. When the enemy tells you you're not good enough, rebuke him. Speak the truth out loud. Memorize passages of Scripture that refer to your newness in Christ and the way God truly sees you, so that you can speak them out loud the next time the accuser tries to tell you you're not good enough.

> God sent him to buy freedom for us who were slaves to the law, so that he could adopt us as his very own children. And because we are his children, God has sent the Spirit of his Son into our hearts, prompting us to call out, "Abba, Father." Now you are no longer a slave but God's own child. And since you are his child, God has made you his heir. (Galatians 4:5–7)

Accept the gift. Righteousness is yours. It is a free gift that comes from faith in Christ, not by works. You can't earn it so there is no room for boasting, pride or self-righteousness. You cannot lose the righteousness of Christ, so there is no need for condemnation when your sin nature wars with your new nature in Christ. When the enemy tries to use either of these schemes to pull you away, remember the truth. The truth sets you free. Your breastplate is made of the impenetrable righteousness of the God of the universe, not your own. Nothing and no one can remove it or take it away.

> I delight greatly in the LORD; my soul rejoices in my God. For he has clothed me with garments of salvation and arrayed me in a robe of his righteousness, as a bridegroom adorns his head like a priest, and as a bride adorns herself with her jewels. (Isaiah 61:10)

Joy in Christ's Righteousness

With each article of God's armor comes the gift of joy. When we find ourselves covered in Christ's righteousness, free from the condemnation and guilt of the sin that used to enslave us, we can be assured that our joy in Him will remain for eternity. In the freedom of His righteousness we can look straight into the eyes of our heavenly Father, never hiding in shame, but coming boldly before His throne with full assurance of His acceptance and love.

Standing in Christ's righteousness, like standing in truth, brings us joy. There we find the freedom that comes only from the wonder of God's never ending forgiveness, in spite of our unworthiness. We can experience true peace, knowing we stand faultless before God. And oh what joy we find as we picture ourselves walking next to the King of Kings, dressed in the pure white robe of *His* righteousness, wearing the crown of the King's child. That is exactly how God sees us.

The Breastplate of Righteousness – Reflections

Key Takeaway:

When we wear Christ's righteousness instead of our own, we are protected by a breastplate Satan's arrows cannot penetrate.

Memory Verse:

"Christ is the end of the law so that there may be righteousness for everyone who believes."

(Romans 10:4)

Notes:

The Breastplate of Righteousness – Study Questions

1. Read Romans 3:20–24 and Isaiah 64:5–7. These verses tell us plainly that we all fall short of the glory of God. Why do you think God cannot be in relationship with imperfect humans?

2. Read Genesis 15:6 and Romans 4:1–5. Even in the Old Testament, God often spoke about righteousness by faith. Why do you think we want to *earn* our salvation when God offers it for free?

3. Read Romans 14:9–12 and Matthew 12:36. How might being "clothed in Christ's righteousness" affect what happens when we stand before God on judgment day?

4. Read Psalm 46:8–11. How does being still and knowing He is God help you to wear His righteousness instead of your own?

5. The enemy uses both self-condemnation and self-righteousness to accuse us. Are there other ways he lies to you or tries to attack you regarding righteousness?

6. How does standing in the righteousness of Christ bring *you* joy?

5

The Shoes of Peace

*But he was pierced for our transgressions, he
was crushed for our iniquities; the punishment
that brought us peace was upon him,
and by his wounds we are healed.*
Isaiah 53:5

The Right Shoes for Battle

God is taking us on quite a journey, isn't He? Can you
believe how far we've come in such a short time? We've
girded our waists with the belt of God's truth and put on
our impenetrable breastplate of Christ's righteousness.
Now it's time to be sure we're wearing the right shoes for
battle. We don't play tennis in dress shoes or run a
marathon in slippers. Neither should we march into battle
without the proper footwear. We must learn to put on the
shoes of peace so we can stand firm.

From the apostle Paul's prison cell, he continued to
write to the church at Ephesus, now looking at the

sandals worn by the Roman soldiers and thinking how those special shoes helped them stand firm in battle. In the earlier years of my walk with Christ, I wasn't quite sure what Paul meant when he said we were to have our "… feet fitted with the readiness that comes from the gospel of peace." (Ephesians 6:15) Then one day, as I was on my way to work, God showed me the meaning of these words in a vivid and personal way.

For a number of years, when my family lived near Chicago, I commuted to work each day by train. I had my routine down pat, leaving early enough to get a good parking spot near the train station in my home town, walking the three or four blocks from my car to the train and then another nine blocks from the train station to my downtown office. It was time-consuming and tiring, but it kept me in shape and provided forty-five minutes of wonderful quiet time on the train to read, study the Bible, journal my prayers, or sometimes just sleep.

On the day of my Ephesians 6:15 lesson, I left the house a bit later than normal, praying I'd find a parking space that wasn't five or six blocks from the station. I got to my favorite parking lot just in time to get one of the very last available spaces, but I was definitely running late so I had to rush to make my train. In the crazy world of commuting, it's not unusual to see men and women loaded down with laptops, purses and other necessities, sprinting three or four blocks to catch the highly coveted express train that shaves a precious fifteen minutes off of the long commute time.

That day I was one of these joggers, running in the rain on sidewalks filled with wet fallen leaves. You can imagine what happened next. In my rush, and having procrastinated on purchasing a good pair of commuter walking shoes, you guessed it; I slipped, twisted my ankle, and fell. I don't remember whether I missed my train or if the Lord was gracious and let me get there on time. But once I did settle into my warm, dry seat, it came to me. I wasn't ready. My feet were not "fitted with the readiness" of the good walking shoes I should have purchased the day I started that job. So what happened? I was taken down. I was injured in the commuter *battle* because I was not prepared with the right shoes to help me *stand firm*. What a vivid picture of our next piece of spiritual armor.

The Ancient Armor – The Warrior's Shoes

The Roman soldiers guarding the apostle Paul wore sandals with thick leather soles embedded with nails or

bits of rock for traction. These sandals, tied to the feet with many leather straps, were well-suited for marching as well as for fighting, and became more comfortable with constant wear.

God's Armor – The Shoes of Peace

In our battle against the powers, authorities and spiritual forces of evil, (Ephesians 6:12) the apostle Paul tells us we must be ready for battle by wearing the correct combat shoes – the gospel of peace. When I had my little mishap on the way to the train that day, God showed me it was clearly no accident that the apostle Paul instructed us to *prepare* ourselves with the *readiness* that comes from proper footwear. I was certainly not ready for running to the train. My feet were fitted with old, inadequate, dress shoes. If I had been ready, I would have been wearing shoes fit for the task. Paul wanted us to know how to get ready for our battle.

The metaphor Paul uses, comparing the soldier's shoes to the gospel of peace, fits perfectly. The sandals worn by the Roman soldiers were sturdy. They were specially made with the ancient version of cleats for stability. The gospel of peace gives us that same kind of solid footing. The good news of Jesus helps us dig in, stand firm, and hold steady in the storms and battles of life. The Roman soldier's sandals became more comfortable for his long marches and dangerous battles the longer they were worn. Our walk with Christ is that way as well. The longer we journey with Him, the more comfortable we become wrapping ourselves in the peace of the gospel. The good news of what Jesus has done for us becomes the most essential part of who we are and how we prepare for everything in life. And just as the Roman soldier's sandals were made for marching and fighting, the gospel of peace steadies us on our daily journey as well as in the heat of battle.

How do the shoes of the gospel of peace ready us for our ongoing battle? We'll answer that question by first taking a look at the armor itself – the gospel of peace. The word *gospel* here in Ephesians 6 is the English translation of the Greek word *euangelion*, which means *good news*. It refers to the good news preached by Jesus that the kingdom of God is at hand (Mark 1:15) as well as the good news of what God has done on behalf of humanity through Christ. (Romans 8:1–2) At the time the New Testament was written, the word *gospel* did not refer to a genre of written literature (the four written gospels) as it does today. Instead, it denoted the verbal message of God's salvation in Jesus Christ on behalf of humankind.[9] Paul is in essence, telling us to get ready for battle by arming ourselves with the good news of Jesus – the gospel of peace.

Why peace? What does the good news of what Christ has done for us have to do with peace? I believe the answer is – everything! Without Christ's payment for our sins at Calvary peace is impossible. Because of the good news of Jesus, we have a supernatural peace that passes all human understanding. (Philippians 4:7) Because of the good news of Jesus, we have peace that no one can take away from us, no matter what our circumstances. (Isaiah 9:7) Do you know that kind of peace? Have you ever felt peace in the midst of strife, pain or even a battle? That is the gospel of peace that comes from Jesus, and only Jesus. That is the peace that allows us to stand when the enemy tries to take us down. We are ready for any onslaught when we stand in the shoes of the gospel of peace.

Let's take some time to look at what the Bible tells us about the peace God gives us through the good news of His Son. The word Paul uses in Ephesians 6:15 translated as *peace* is from the Greek *eirēnē*, which means harmony, tranquility or freedom from worry.[10] Oh how wonderful those words sound, don't they? Life would be a lot easier if we could just have freedom from worry. Yet, God's Word says peace is not just something we hope for, it is something we already have. (John 14:27) We are told the spiritual blessing of true peace is a gift from God. In the same way that the belt of truth and the breastplate of righteousness do not come from within *us*, the assurance and firm foundation we have wearing our shoes of peace do not come from anything within ourselves. Our armor is the peace that comes only through the gospel of Jesus Christ. We can't invent or create peace that endures. We can't *positive think* ourselves into a peace that passes understanding. But the peace we receive from God, as part of His gift of salvation, is a peace that holds us firm and allows us to be ready for any attack the enemy can launch at us. Let's look at what God's Word says about peace.

God is a God of peace. He sent His Son to earth to bring us peace. But the truth is Jesus told us the peace He brings us is going to be different from what we expect. It's a lasting peace, an internal peace with Him that is available even when war and disaster are all around us.

> For God is not a God of disorder but of peace.
> (1 Corinthians 14:33)

Peace comes through Jesus Christ. Our only pathway to the peace God offers is through His Son, Jesus. His forgiveness alone reconciles us with God and allows us to share in His true peace.

> Therefore, since we have been justified through faith, we have peace with God through our Lord Jesus Christ. (Romans 5:1)

The world cannot give us peace. Worldly peace is temporary. It can never last. It is shallow and shaky and will disappear at the first sign of trouble. But in Christ, we can experience peace even through the attacks of our enemy, Satan.

> I have told you these things, so that in me you may have peace. In this world you will have trouble. But take heart! I have overcome the world. (John 16:33)

God offers peace in all circumstances. True peace is not dependent on peaceful circumstances in our lives. With the peace that fills our souls as children walking with our Savior, we can rest, even though the world around us seems to be in turmoil.

> Do not be anxious about anything, but in every situation, by prayer and petition, with thanks-giving, present your requests to God. And the peace of God, which transcends all under-standing, will guard your hearts and your minds in Christ Jesus. (Philippians 4:6-7)

Christ did not come to bring peace with others. Although Christ did come to bring us peace with God and peace within our own hearts, He never promised we would have peace with other people. As a matter of fact, Jesus told us clearly that we would experience just the opposite. Our relationship with God often brings division in families, as well as between friends and co-workers.

Do not suppose that I have come to bring peace to the earth. I did not come to bring peace, but a sword. For I have come to turn a man against his father, a daughter against her mother, a daughter-in-law against her mother-in-law – a man's enemies will be the members of his own household. (Matthew 10:34–36)

With the true peace that comes from the good news of salvation in Jesus, the enemy cannot overcome us. Satan can't make us afraid or lure us into the futile attempt to attain holiness on our own. When we put on our battle shoes, the gospel of peace, and never forget what Christ has done for us, we stand firm – feet on solid ground – never slipping, never falling, always standing in Christ as victorious warriors. For that very reason, because he knows how much freedom and joy the peace of Jesus gives, our enemy wants to take it away. It's time once again for us to uncover our enemy's tactics and schemes, to see how he tries to defeat us by taking away our peace.

Satan's Schemes Against Peace

As we have seen so many times before, the enemy cannot really steal the gifts and promises of our mighty God unless we let him. God's truth, our righteousness in Christ, and the peace that comes from the good news of

Jesus, are our inheritance as children of God. But the enemy can make us think we are orphans. He lies, manipulates and deceives his way into our hearts and minds until we no longer even see the unparalleled gifts that are ours through our relationship with Christ. What is his strategy to take away our peace? How does he get us to wear the wrong shoes so we trip and fall on our journey toward heaven?

Satan does not have to look far to find the potholes and rocks he needs to send us stumbling to the ground. Jesus warned us we would have trouble in this world. If we keep our eyes on the world and the troubles of our lives, we will very quickly be overcome by the feeling that there is no peace to be found anywhere. That is the lie Satan wants us to believe. His plan is to keep us focused on our problems, so that the *peace that passes understanding* will simply pass us by. What does the enemy use to take our minds and hearts off the peace God gives through our assurances in Christ?

Satan uses fear. It's hard to find peace when we are steeped in fear. The Bible repeatedly tells us we are to fear God only. The holy fear of God is not terror. The New Bible Dictionary tells us *holy fear* "is God-given, enabling men to reverence God's authority, obey his command-ments and hate and shun all form of evil."[11] But the fears our enemy uses to steal our peace are ungodly fears, like fear of man (1 Samuel 15:24) and fear of punishment (Hebrews 10:27). Ungodly fears overwhelm (Exodus 15:15–16) and destroy (Psalm 73:19). Guilt can produce ungodly fear. (Proverbs 28:1) These kinds of fear lead to chronic anxiety, phobias and even cause us to stop trusting in the God who brings us peace. Don't let the enemy use his tool of fear against you. Put on your shoes of peace and stand firm in the promises of a loving and powerful God. Remember what Jesus has done for you. Christ died to take away the one thing we should fear most, eternal death. We no longer need to fear the loss of our eternal relationship with our Father in heaven.

> For you did not receive a spirit that makes you a slave again to fear, but you received the Spirit of sonship. And by him we cry, "Abba, Father." (Romans 8:15)

Satan uses worry. Although worry is closely related to fear, in reality there is a significant difference. Worry does not always mean being afraid. Often the enemy just uses our lack of trust and our need to control our circumstances to create a lifestyle of worry. We can worry about anything and everything and when we do, we have chosen to give up our peace. We worry about good things almost as much as bad. We worry about what to wear to a social event. We worry about our children's grades. We worry about getting to church on time. We worry about doing well in a presentation for work. In some of these instances, our worry either ends up in fear or was caused by fear in the first place. But often, the enemy is satisfied with just making us believe God is not in control and cannot be trusted. There are forty-seven verses in the Bible that include the word "worry" and *every* one of them tells us … *"Don't."* Worry is a waste of time, energy and joy, and it is direct disobedience to God's Word. No wonder the enemy wants to keep us in a state of constant worry – it's a great way to steal our peace.

> Don't worry about anything; instead, pray about everything. Tell God what you need, and thank him for all he has done. Then you will experience God's peace, which exceeds anything we can understand. His peace will guard your hearts and minds as you live in Christ Jesus. (Philippians 4:6–7 NLT)

Satan uses doubt. There is a reason God tells us not to doubt or persist in unbelief. Doubt takes away our joy, our assurance and our peace. Doubt makes us question the truth of God's Word and, at times, even makes us question the very goodness of God. Planting seeds of doubt has been one of the enemy's most powerful tools since he first deceived Eve in the Garden of Eden. (Genesis 3:1) And what does Satan do after he sows doubtful thoughts into our minds? He condemns us for having those very doubts. He questions our salvation, telling us we can't *really* be saved if we doubt. But the truth is believers throughout history have had doubts. In the Old Testament Moses (Exodus 5:22–23), Gideon (Judges 6:13), and Joshua (Joshua 7:7–8) all questioned God and doubted what He had told them. Even Jesus' own disciples doubted and questioned Him. (Mark 6:37; John 20:25; Luke 24:25)

God wants us to trust Him and to reject the doubts that sometimes fill our minds. He knows they steal our peace. God gives us abundant life (John 10:10) when we believe Him and live in the truth. So don't let the enemy steal the peace that is yours in Christ by believing or dwelling on the doubts he plants in your mind and heart. Ask God to help you overcome your doubts. (Mark 9:24) Let your doubt push you into God's Word. Hold fast to the truth. Remember what God has done for you. Believe God and take Him at His word. Focus your mind on what you *know* is true. Don't let the things you don't understand get in the way of the rock-solid truths you have based your life on. Take your thoughts captive to Christ, and hold tightly to His peace – the peace that passes understanding.

> Then Peter got down out of the boat, walked on the water and came toward Jesus. But when he saw the wind, he was afraid and, beginning to sink, cried out, "Lord, save me!" Immediately

> Jesus reached out his hand and caught him. "You of little faith," he said, "why did you doubt?" (Matthew 14:29–31)

Satan uses trials. It is hard to hold fast to our peace when we're suffering through extremely difficult or painful circumstances. We want to have faith, to let God carry us, and even hope He will make some good come from our struggles, but often we allow the enemy's lies to fill our minds and take away our hope and our peace. In our most trying times, Satan whispers lies into our minds like, "How can God love you if He allows you to go through this?" Or "You must have done something to make God angry, or He wouldn't let this happen to you." Or even, "God doesn't care about you or your circumstances." These and so many other lies often go rushing through our minds during trying times – and who doesn't have difficult times? How often do we allow our peace to be shattered because of our circumstances?

That is exactly what the enemy wants. He doesn't have to do much to orchestrate the trouble, although he certainly can and probably often does. But Satan often attempts to use our trials to pull us away from God. He wants to make us believe God has forsaken us when we can't see His mighty hand relieving us from our pain and suffering. The truth is God is present *in the midst of* our suffering. It is in pain that we see Him most clearly and hear His voice most unmistakably. In his book, *The Problem of Pain*, C.S. Lewis says these famous words: "God whispers to us in our pleasures, speaks in our conscience, but shouts in our pains: it is his megaphone to rouse a deaf world."[12] God never leaves us. He is right there with us in both the good times and in the fire. If we let Him speak to us in our pain instead of listening to the lying voice of the enemy, we will find victory, peace and yes, even joy in the midst of our trials.

> In all this you greatly rejoice, though now for a little while you may have had to suffer grief in all kinds of trials. These have come so that the proven genuineness of your faith – of greater worth than gold, which perishes even though refined by fire – may result in praise, glory and honor when Jesus Christ is revealed.
> (1 Peter 1:6–7)

Satan uses prosperity. Finally, let me say just a word about one more tool Satan uses to get us to run our race in the wrong kind of shoes. Peace comes from our relationship and security in Christ. But sometimes, instead of trying to use our trials and negative thoughts to pull us away from our source of peace, he uses our good times and self-sufficiency. If Satan can't steal our peace by getting us to doubt, fear, or worry, he often lures us away from the Source of our peace and joy by making life so good we don't think we need God. Be very careful. In hard times and in times of plenty, look to your Savior for your joy and peace. Worldly peace is deceiving and fleeting. The good times we enjoy today can be gone in the blink of an eye. Hold tight to the real peace you find in the good news of Jesus.

> Let them no longer fool themselves by trusting in empty riches, for emptiness will be their only reward. (Job 15:31)

We've examined only a few of the many ways our enemy tries to steal the peace God wants to gives us as His children. But we have nothing to fear. We can arm ourselves for this battle. Let's look now at some of the practical ways we can put on our shoes of peace.

Putting On the Shoes of Peace

As we've seen, the enemy uses so many of life's circumstances, both good and bad, as well as our own emotions to keep us from living in the peace God gives through His Son. Fear, worry, doubts, trials and even prosperity threaten to take our true peace and joy if we let them. So how do we wear the right shoes for battle? How do we ensure we won't get knocked to the ground because we have failed to ready ourselves with the gospel of peace?

Know what true peace is. True peace is not the absence of trials or turmoil in our lives, but the experience of walking in God's plan in the midst of anything this world or the enemy can throw at us. Never get the *feeling* of peace mixed up with true peace. What we feel is often false. It is just our earthly reaction to our circumstances. Remember, true peace comes in knowing we are loved by the God who created us, and that in Jesus, no one or nothing can ever separate us from God's love.

> Let the peace of Christ rule in your hearts, since as members of one body you were called to peace. (Colossians 3:15)

Remember where peace comes from. True peace comes only from God. If we look to the world for peace, we will find only temporary respite. The joys and pleasures of this life are often swept away in a nanosecond by tragedy, trial, illness or pain. But the peace that comes to us through Jesus Christ endures through anything. That peace is the gift of our eternal, unchanging Father, and it can never ever be taken from us.

> I have told you these things, so that in me you may have peace. In this world you will have trouble. But take heart! I have overcome the world. (John 16:33)

Cling to peace, not prosperity. All the good things this world has to offer are gifts from God. While prosperity and a good life are not sinful, they can easily become our gods. When we depend on money, a nice house, a good job or human relationships to bring us peace and even joy, we rely on things that are shallow and often short-lived. Earthly peace and prosperity can be drowned in the flood of tribulation or can become for us a never ending pursuit that takes us far away from God's will and His purpose for our lives.

> But seek first his kingdom and his righteousness,
> and all these things will be given to you as well.
> (Matthew 6:33)

Walk closely to the One who brings peace. The peace we have in God is ours because of the gospel, the good news of what Christ did for us at Calvary. Stay close to your Source of peace. Stay close to the One who *is* your peace. When the enemy fills your mind with lies that would take you far from the peace of God, be sure you are so close to Christ that it only takes a second for your mind and heart to feel His arms of love around you and to hear God's voice saying, "You are mine. I bought you with a price. I will never leave you or forsake you. Peace, my peace I give you." Remember, when you draw near to God, He draws near to you. (James 4:8) Your peace is found in Him.

But as for me, it is good to be near God. I have made the Sovereign LORD my refuge; I will tell of all your deeds. (Psalm 73:28)

Peace – The Soul's Doorway to Joy

It always amazes me how God gives us exactly what we need when we need it. Just a week before I began writing this chapter, my soul was nourished by these astounding words from the wonderful little devotional, *Jesus Calling* by Sarah Young.

> Peace be with you! Ever since the resurrection, this has been My watchword to those who yearn for Me. As you sit quietly, let My Peace settle over you and enfold you in My loving Presence. To provide this radiant Peace for you, I died a criminal's death. Receive My Peace abundantly and thankfully. It is a rare treasure, dazzling in delicate beauty yet strong enough to withstand all onslaughts. Wear My Peace with regal dignity. It will keep your heart and mind close to Mine. [13]

Jesus truly was calling *me* that day. And He calls to each and every one of us every day. That, my friend, is true peace and joy. When I live in the knowledge that God is with me, that He loves me unconditionally and has paid the price for my sin, that I am His child, I have peace and joy. When I remember He hears my every cry and already knows how He is going to use my hard times to bring me closer to Him, I have peace and joy. And, when I bask in the peace that passes understanding, then I also experience *inexpressible* joy.

> You love him even though you have never seen him. Though you do not see him now, you trust him; and you rejoice with a glorious, inexpressible joy. (1 Peter 1:8)

The Shoes of Peace – Reflections

Key Takeaway:

When we put on our battle shoes, the gospel of peace, and never forget what Christ has done for us, we stand firm – feet on solid ground – never slipping, never falling, always standing in Christ as victorious warriors.

Memory Verse:

"I have told you these things, so that in me you may have peace. In this world you will have trouble. But take heart! I have overcome the world." (John 16:33)

Notes:

The Shoes of Peace – Study Questions

1. Read Ephesians 6:15. How does the gospel, the good news of Jesus, bring you peace in your daily life? How does the peace of the gospel give you readiness for your battle with the enemy?

2. Read John 14:25–27. How is the peace of Christ different from worldly peace? In what ways do you find yourself looking to the world for peace?

3. Read Matthew 10:34–36 and 1 Thessalonians 5:23. If God is a God of peace, why do you think Jesus told us He did not come to bring peace but a sword?

4. Read John 10:10. The "thief" in this verse is Satan himself, who tries to steal everything God gives us, including our peace. How does the thief steal your peace? How can you stop him?

5. Do you find yourself closer or farther from God in good times?

6. In this chapter I listed four ways to put on the shoes of peace. Can you think of any other ways to put on Christ's peace?

7. Write a few sentences about how you find peace and joy in the midst of your trials.

6

The Shield of Faith

*Against all hope, Abraham in hope believed
and so became the father of many nations.*
Romans 4:18

Protection from Flaming Arrows

Is your armor getting heavy yet? Mine isn't either. Since
this armor we wear belongs to God, and is given to us as
a gift, it is not burdensome. "For my yoke is easy and my
burden is light." (Matthew 11:30) We've already put on
three very important protective coverings – the belt of
truth, the breastplate of righteousness and the shoes of
peace. Now it's time to examine another piece of our
armor – one that would be extremely heavy if it didn't
belong to God. Let's take a close look at the *shield of faith*.

Ephesians 6:16 says, "In addition to all this, take up
the shield of faith, with which you can extinguish all the
flaming arrows of the evil one." Here, the apostle Paul
not only tells us to take up our battle shield, but he also

describes exactly what we're fighting against – *the flaming arrows of the evil one*. I believe Paul's intention was to give us a strong and clear warning that our Christian faith will, most certainly, be under attack. I don't know how you experience this spiritual war in your life, but I can tell you, at times I truly feel like I am ducking and bobbing to avoid the onslaught of Satan's arrows. Thank God for the protection of His marvelous gift – His shield of faith.

The Ancient Armor – The Warrior's Shield

The shield of a Roman soldier was made of wood. It was about two-and-a-half feet wide and four feet long and was

overlaid with linen and leather to beat out fires or extinguish flaming arrows tipped with blazing tar. The curve in the shield was created using three bonded layers of thin wood strips. A bronze rim covered the rounded edges as additional protection. The shield protected the Roman soldier's whole body and linked with other warriors' shields to drive a wedge for advance, or to form walls for defense.[14]

God's Armor – The Shield of Faith

Once again it's remarkable to see how appropriately the apostle Paul compares each piece of physical armor to our spiritual weapons. The Roman soldier's shield covered their whole body. Our faith is just like that shield. Faith covers every part of our lives. Wherever we are under attack, any place in our lives where we are vulnerable to our enemy's lies and schemes, our faith in the God who loves us is the overarching protection that will keep us safe.

And isn't it interesting how the shields the Roman soldiers carried were used to join them together, arm in arm, giving them added protection and strength that they did not have by themselves? That is exactly what our faith does. When we link arm in arm with our fellow believers, we are stronger and more powerful because of our shared faith. No wonder the enemy's schemes seek to separate us not only from God, but also from each other.

We need to take up our shield of faith and never lay it down. Even when the enemy's deceit and attacks make it feel too heavy to carry, we must hold firm to the faith that saved us, the faith that keeps us strong. What does that kind of faith look like? What kind of faith shields us from attack? How do we have faith that moves mountains and gives us the power to walk on water? Hebrews 11:1 says, "Now faith is being sure of what we hope for and certain of what we do not see." Let's take a closer look at what God's Word says about that kind of faith.

By faith we are adopted into God's family. When we choose to believe and follow Jesus, we are given the awesome gift of salvation, forgiveness for all our sin, and the unsurpassable joy of living in Christ's righteousness as one of God's own family. Our position as royal children is secure because of our faith in what Christ did for us on the cross.

> Yet to all who did receive him, to those who believed in his name, he gave the right to become children of God – children born not of natural descent, nor of human decision or a husband's will, but born of God. (John 1:12–13)

Faith is a gift. We don't create the faith that is in our hearts. It is a gift given by our loving Father God. However, we can seek it and develop it. Often we must *choose* to have faith, even when the enemy tries to tell us the Lord God in whom we've put our trust is no longer trustworthy. Those lies will destroy us and others around us. Know that God, who planted the seed of faith in us from the beginning, will in fact hold us up and continue to strengthen our faith, if we ask Him.

For by the grace given me I say to every one of you: Do not think of yourself more highly than you ought, but think of yourself with sober judgment, according to the measure of faith God has given you. (Romans 12:3 BSB)

Through faith we receive the Holy Spirit and His gifts. God bestows so many wonderful blessings and rewards upon those who have faith in Him. One of the most powerful is the indwelling of the Holy Spirit (the Spirit of God, actually living within you) and the blessing of His spiritual gifts. Our lives are changed when we receive the sweet fruit of the Spirit that is available to us as believers. Galatians 5:22-23 says this: "But the fruit of the Spirit is love, joy, peace, forbearance, kindness, goodness, faithfulness, gentleness and self-control." What a difference we would see in our lives if we received and exercised these incredible gifts. Ask Christ to fill you to overflowing with His Spirit, to build your faith and give you power that is impossible on your own – power to obey, power to believe, power to desire what God desires, power to love like Jesus loves.

> Peter replied, "Repent and be baptized, every one of you, in the name of Jesus Christ for the forgiveness of your sins. And you will receive the gift of the Holy Spirit. The promise is for you and your children and for all who are far off

– for all whom the Lord our God will call."
(Acts 2:38-39)

Faith gives us strength to overcome the enemy.
Without faith Satan can control your mind, your heart and your soul. Your faith in Jesus Christ gives you salvation, adoption into God's family, and the power to stand firm against the lies and schemes of the devil. With faith, we can and will overcome the enemy every time.

> Be alert and of sober mind. Your enemy the devil prowls around like a roaring lion looking for someone to devour. Resist him, standing firm in the faith, because you know that the family of believers throughout the world is undergoing the same kind of sufferings.
> (1 Peter 5:8–9)

Faith brings healing. In New Testament times, Jesus and His disciples healed the sick, freed the demon-possessed, and even raised the dead. Why? Because of their faith. I believe Jesus continues to heal today, both spiritually and physically. Remember, God does not change. Hebrews 13:8 tells us, "Jesus Christ is the same yesterday and today and forever." If Jesus healed those who had enough faith to believe while He walked on this earth, and gave His disciples power to do the same, what would make us think He does not have the same power and desire to heal today?

> By faith in the name of Jesus, this man whom you see and know was made strong. It is Jesus' name and the faith that comes through him that has given this complete healing to him, as you can all see. (Acts 3:16)

Our Faith will be tested. In *Be Available, An Old Testament Study*, Warren Wiersbe says this about the testing of our faith: "A faith that can't be tested can't be trusted. God allows our faith to be tested for at least two reasons: first, to show us whether our faith is real or counterfeit, and second, to strengthen our faith for the tasks He has set before us. God often puts us through the valley of testing before allowing us to reach the mountain peak of victory. Charles Spurgeon was right when he said that the promises of God shine brightest in the furnace of affliction, and it is in claiming those promises that we gain the victory."[15]

> Consider it pure joy, my brothers and sisters, whenever you face trials of many kinds, because you know that the testing of your faith produces perseverance. Let perseverance finish its work so that you may be mature and complete, not lacking anything. (James 1:2–4)

There is so much more we could say – filling up page after page with truth, gifts and blessings bestowed upon us when we have faith in God and His precious Son. Our faith covers, protects, and shields us from the destruction the enemy can cause by pulling us away from God and each other. Satan will relentlessly attack our faith. He shoots flaming arrows that would pierce our hearts, minds and souls if our shield was made of *anything less* than our faith in a powerful and mighty God.

Satan's Schemes Against Faith

Satan's primary weapon against our faith is the same now as it was in the Garden of Eden – doubt. In the garden, he said to Eve, "Did God really say, 'You must not eat from any tree in the garden?'" (Genesis 3:1) Our enemy loves casting doubt upon everything we believe and know to be true about God. Remember, Satan knows he cannot have us. We are children of God, adopted into His family for eternity. So the enemy's schemes against believers are aimed at making our faith useless and rendering us powerless to do the will of our Father. He wants to stop us from being effective for Christ and bringing anyone else into the kingdom. What better way to do that than to make us question our faith? Let's look at some of the fiery arrows the enemy launches to bring our faith into question and plant seeds of doubt that could cause us to stop living for God.

Questioning God's goodness. If Satan can make us believe God is not good and therefore cannot be trusted, he can take away not only our joy, but also the power and witness of the gospel in our lives. So our enemy plants seeds of doubt like these: "If God is so good, why did He let that little baby die?" or "If God is so good, why does He allow natural disasters to kill thousands of innocent people?" or even "If God is so good, how could He send good people to hell just because they grew up with a different religion?"

Do any of these sound familiar? They not only are asked by unbelievers every day, but they also go through the minds of good, solid Christians who have been loving and serving God for decades. Human logic cannot answer all the questions that go through our minds or that others may ask. Our God's ways are infinitely greater than we can possibly comprehend. (Isaiah 55:9) And we know our faith must not depend upon our human understanding of an inexplicable God. When the enemy plants this kind of doubt, remember everything you *know* to be true about God. Look at your own life and counter the enemy's lies and doubt-producing questions with the truth of what God has done for you. Choose to focus on the ways He has proven Himself faithful and good in your life.

Questioning God's promises. The first recorded words of our enemy, Satan, were "Did he *really* say ..." That is exactly what he continues to say to us today. Did God *really* say that eternal life is a gift to us? Did God *really* promise never to leave us or forsake us? And if He did, where is He now in the midst of my trials and pain? Did God *really* say He'd forgive even that sin?

There was a time in my life when I went through some extremely difficult circumstances. I was falling apart emotionally, and spiritually I was questioning everything I thought I believed. I searched desperately for God during those turbulent days, and remember vividly the day God used this verse to pierce my heart with truth.

> Against all hope, Abraham in hope believed and so became the father of many nations, just as it had been said to him, "So shall your offspring be." Without weakening in his faith, he faced the fact that his body was as good as dead – since he was about a hundred years old – and that Sarah's womb was also dead. Yet he did not waver through unbelief regarding the promise of God, but was strengthened in his faith and gave glory to God, being fully persuaded that God had power to do what he had promised.
> (Romans 4:18–21)

That passage just about leapt off the page at me. It reminded me that even though things seemed hopeless at the time, I, like Abraham, who *faced the fact that his body was as good as dead* could count on the fact that *God had power to do what He had promised.* But then the critical question came to me. I thought, "Abraham knew what God promised him, but what exactly has God promised *me?*" That sent me on a search, a quest to learn what God truly had promised me. And oh what a journey it was! During that terrible – wonderful time, I experienced an intimacy with God I had never before believed possible.

When the enemy plants doubts in your mind and says, *"Did he really say …?"* seek and find the promises your loving Father makes to you. We must *know* the truth. We can cling to God's promises only when we know what they are. And we can fight the lies of the enemy when we know Who has made the promises we cling to.

Questioning God's existence. If we are honest, I think most of us would say there have been times in our Christian life when we've wondered if everything we believe is true. And sometimes we even hear a voice in our head saying, "Come on. This God you have given your life to is invisible – get real!" If you have not had that kind of doubt you have reason to be very thankful, but I confess; I have. Our enemy's deception is powerful. There are times when he is able to sneak in a thought that goes completely contrary to what we know to be true and what we have staked our faith and our lives upon for years. When that happens, we must cling to the truth and choose to take God at His word. We must look to the Bible and fill our minds with the truth of God. And we must also look to the evidence of God in our own lives.

Remember all the ways God has moved miraculously in other people's lives and in your own. Consider all the things He has done for you, your family and your friends. Write them down. Journaling is a wonderful tool for this. It not only gives us a way to focus completely on God while we are praying in written form, but it also gives us a record of God's work in our lives to look back on when times are hard. That is exactly what the Bible is, a record of God's movement and hand in the lives of mankind and specifically, His chosen people. We can continue the written story when we journal our prayers and life events. Remember. There is a reason God's Word tells us over and over again to remember His deeds. This is how we know He is who He says He is. When the enemy puts crazy thoughts in your mind, sometimes even doubting God's very existence, say "Get behind me Satan!" (Matthew 16:23; Mark 8:33) And remember everything your awesome, powerful, invisible God has done for you.

Questioning the truth of the Bible. Another way the enemy undermines our faith is by tempting us to question the truth of God's Word. Many people do not believe the Bible is the inerrant Word of God. They say it is folklore handed down generation after generation – simply fables and stories that teach good principles to live by. These people deny the Bible was inspired by God. Satan loves that lie.

The enemy not only uses people with different viewpoints to make us question our beliefs, but he also uses difficult Bible passages as well. The fact is, Scripture was written thousands of years ago in a language and style very different from our own. So what do we do when God's Word is confusing? What do we do when one passage appears to contradict another? First, bring it to God. Ask Him to show you the truth.

Then, search out the truth. Many online Bible study tools and commentaries are available to help us understand the meaning and context of what we read in Scripture. Study more than one version of the Bible. Often reading a more modern translation can help clarify the meaning of the text. Jeremiah 29:13 says "You will seek me and find me when you seek me with all your heart." So seek Him. Seek truth. Let your doubts and questions push you *to* God, not away from Him.

When the enemy tempts you to doubt Scripture, remember *everything* you know to be true. Ask yourself these questions, and write down your answers! What do you know to be true about Jesus? About God? About Salvation? Faith? Forgiveness? Yourself? About this life and the next? What do you know to be true about the enemy?

Focus on what you *know* is true, and ask God to open your eyes and your mind to reveal His truth about the things that confuse you or make you doubt. God is faithful. He will give you wisdom. "If any of you lacks wisdom, he should ask God, who gives generously to all without finding fault, and it will be given to him." (James 1:5)

Taking Up the Shield of Faith

Now that we have seen many of the ways our enemy shoots his flaming arrows to defeat our faith, it's time once again to discover what we need to do to *take up* and hold on to our shield. Remember, our faith is a gift. We receive it from God, but we hold it tight with our own free will and the strength given to us by the very Spirit of God. So what can we do to hold our shield of faith and never drop it?

Ask God to increase your faith. God loves to give to His children when we ask according to His will. And God's will is that we would have faith to move mountains! So go ahead... ask.

> The apostles said to the Lord, "Increase our faith!" (Luke 17:5)

Be sincere in your faith. Don't be afraid to admit to God when you are unsure or doubting. He knows your thoughts anyway. When you are sincere and honest with God, He can and will help you overcome your unbelief.

> The goal of this command is love, which comes from a pure heart and a good conscience and a sincere faith. (1 Timothy 1:5)

Stand fast in your faith. Remember, in this battle we're fighting, the enemy is going to shoot his flaming arrows right at your heart – at the very faith that made you a child of the King.

> Be on your guard; stand firm in the faith; be courageous; be strong. (1 Corinthians 16:13)

Be strong in your faith. Let God make you strong in your faith. We can't do that by ourselves any more than we can save ourselves. God will strengthen our faith as we seek Him, obey Him and hold on to His promises.

> Yet he did not waver through unbelief regarding the promise of God, but was strengthened in his faith and gave glory to God, being fully persuaded that God had power to do what he had promised. (Romans 4:20–21)

Stand with other people of faith. Just as the Roman soldiers linked their shields together to form a wall of protection and a strong wedge to press through to defeat their enemies, so too, we need to link our shield of faith with other believers for strength and protection. God never meant for us to live our Christian lives alone. There is power in the faith of the saints joined in belief, worship and prayer.

> Though one may be overpowered, two can defend themselves. A cord of three strands is not quickly broken. (Ecclesiastes 4:12)

Choose to have faith. Choose to believe. When your life is in turmoil or the enemy has succeeded in putting doubts in your mind, *choose* to believe – again and again. Faith is a gift God has given you. No one can steal your shield of faith, but you can willingly put it down. You must *decide* to never let it go.

> Let us hold unswervingly to the hope we profess, for he who promised is faithful. (Hebrews 10:23)

Faith – The Essential Foundation of Joy

I love the apostle Paul's conclusion after he weighed the joy of dying and being with God, against the mission of staying on earth a little longer to continue in the work

God had given him. Paul said, "… I am convinced that I will remain alive so I can continue to help all of you grow and experience the joy of your faith." (Philippians 1:25 NLT) Oh how I pray that we too will grow and experience the *joy* of our faith, because faith truly is the foundation of our joy. Without faith, there is no lasting joy. Oh, we can surely find some happiness in the things of this earth, but it is so fleeting. Yet in faith, holding to the truth and power of God's Word and to His Son, we have the kind of joy that lasts through all the trials and triumphs of our lives.

Hold on to your shield of faith, my friends. Hold on to the joy that is yours through your faith in the God of creation. Joy is the result of a relationship with the King. In the midst of this battle we fight, remember who you are, and find joy in the faith that has made you the child of the most-high God!

The Shield of Faith – Reflections

Key Takeaway:

Faith is a gift God has given you. No one can steal your shield of faith, but you can willingly put it down.

Memory Verse:

"Now faith is being sure of what we hope for and certain of what we do not see." (Hebrews 11:1)

Notes:

The Shield of Faith – Study Questions

1. Read Hebrews 11:6. This verse says without faith it's impossible to please God. And 1 John 3:23 tells us it is God's command that we believe in Jesus. These are very strong statements. Why do you think God wants so much for us to have faith?

2. Read Matthew 14:26–33 and James 1:5–7. Jesus was patient with those who doubted, and asks us to be merciful to those who doubt. (Jude 1:22) How do you think God feels about our doubts? Why do you think James said "he who doubts is like a wave of the sea, blown and tossed by the wind"?

3. What is the doubt Satan most frequently puts in your mind to threaten your faith? How can you hold up your shield to deflect that *specific* arrow?

4. Read James 1:2–4. God's Word speaks frequently of our faith being tested. Why do you think God tests our faith? In what ways has *your* faith been tested? What did God teach you, or do in you or for you, through your testing?

5. Read 1 Peter 1:8-9. Theses passages tell us our faith brings "an inexpressible and glorious joy." How has God brought joy to you through your faith? How is that joy different than happiness?

7

The Helmet of Salvation

But since we belong to the day, let us be
self-controlled, putting on faith and love as a
breastplate, and the hope of salvation as a helmet.
1 Thessalonians 5:8

God's Protective Head-gear

In an earlier chapter I mentioned that my family and I
lived in the Chicago area for many years, where winters
can be downright frigid. During a few of those years, I
commuted via train from the suburbs into the "Windy
City" for work each day. I had a long walk once I got off
the train, so in those wintry months I wore a favorite hat
that covered not only my head, but also my ears and neck
to protect me from bitter winds. When it was really cold –
I mean the kind of twenty-degrees-below-zero cold that
takes your breath away and freezes your eyeballs – I could
even pull the thick ties that normally covered my ears and
neck, all the way across my nose and mouth for
protection from the stinging cold wind.

Now *that* was protective head-gear. Of course for some, other examples of protective head covering might come to mind, for example a football helmet, a bicycle or motorcycle helmet, or a goalie's mask. But for me, the picture of my mega-winter-hat hits home. It helps me think of our next piece of spiritual armor as real protection, a covering that shields more than just the head. Our *helmet of salvation* does far more than that. It literally gives us life. Let's begin our journey to discover the life-changing truth about salvation by once again looking at the soldier's armor as the apostle Paul saw it from his Roman prison cell in approximately 60 A.D.

The Ancient Armor – The Warrior's Helmet

The Roman soldier's iron helmet was forged from one piece of metal and lined with leather to protect the head. Plates hung down along the cheeks and another plate protected the back of the neck and shoulders. Crests made of dyed horsehair indicated rank.

The helmet was made to protect the part of the human body that controls life itself, the brain. The Romans knew that in battle a warrior might survive the loss of a limb or even the piercing of the body, but damaging the brain could mean the end of a soldier's life or, at the very least, the end of his fighting days.

God's Armor – The Helmet of Salvation

We've talked quite a bit already about how our minds must be guarded from the attacks of the enemy. Satan knows that our thoughts control our emotions, our moods and even our actions, and those in turn affect our relationships with others and with God. No wonder the apostle Paul saw the soldier's helmet as a perfect metaphor for another critical piece of armor necessary to fight this battle for our minds. The symbol of a helmet is used to represent salvation in a number of Scripture passages. You will find it in Isaiah 59:17, 1 Thessalonians 5:8 and in Ephesians 6:17, which says, "Take the helmet of salvation and the sword of the Spirit, which is the word of God."

I believe the writers of Scripture spoke frequently about the helmet of salvation because this gift is the core of what we believe and the foundation of God's work in our lives. Our sin separates us from God. We are lost and dying, and we cannot rescue ourselves. But God's plan from the beginning of time, even before the Garden of Eden, was to physically step into human history, walk with us, teach us and die for us in order to provide the salvation that only His death could purchase.

It was not by accident that the apostle Paul used the helmet as his word picture for salvation. Coming from his personal background as a Pharisee, a religious leader, (Philippians 3:3–5) Paul had studied the writings of the prophet Isaiah. I imagine as he wrote to the believers at Ephesus, he was remembering Isaiah 59:17: "He put on righteousness as his breastplate, and the helmet of salvation on his head." After teaching and living under the strict requirements of the law of Moses, surely Paul fully understood and embraced the truth of salvation by faith in Jesus, which was heresy to his fellow Pharisees, but life to those who knew Christ. Certainly he was fully aware of his need to protect his own mind from the accusations and lies that would be hurled at him by the father of lies himself, through the very people he once taught alongside.

Paul risked everything to preach the gospel, the good news of Jesus. Salvation *is* the good news. Jesus left His rightful place on the throne of God to become a human being and suffered a criminal's death to save us. (Philippians 2:6–8) Salvation is the reason we can stand before our holy God and call Him *Abba* – or Daddy.

The *Dictionary of Bible Themes* speaks of salvation this way: "Salvation is the transformation of a person's individual nature and relationship with God as a result of repentance and faith in the atoning death of Jesus Christ on the cross. All humanity stands in need of salvation, which is only possible through faith in Jesus Christ. Salvation involves a change in the relationship between God and a person. Salvation includes God's adoption of believers into his family, his acceptance of them as righteous and his forgiveness of their sins. It also includes personal renewal and transformation through the work of the Holy Spirit."[16]

Never forget salvation is free – but it was anything but cheap. It cost the Son of God *everything*! I pray we will never become so familiar with Christ's sacrifice that we lose our awe and thankful hearts for His remarkable gift. Let's now move ahead and uncover what God's Word tells us about the amazing truth of salvation, and how it protects us against the enemy's attacks on our minds.

We All Need Salvation

We cannot have a discussion about the helmet of salvation without first acknowledging that every human being who ever lived or ever will live needs a Savior. Why? Because "all have sinned and fall short of the glory of God." (Romans 3:23)

Sin is part of our nature. God created Adam and Eve as perfect children, made in His own likeness. But ever since our first parents let Satan's lies influence their thinking and chose to use God's gift of free will to disobey Him, we have all inherited their sin nature. It's in our DNA. If you don't believe that, just watch a two-year-old in the supermarket willfully defying his mother or having a temper tantrum because he's not getting what he wants. That child hasn't *learned* to be a sinner; he was born with rebellion, defiance and self-will as part of his very being.

The problem is many people don't believe they are sinners and therefore see no need for a Savior. In our culture we are taught that man is basically good, and his sin (if we even dare call it that in this day of political correctness) comes from what he has experienced in life. We make excuses for unrighteous behavior, blaming much of it on our upbringing and environment, or comparing it to the sin of others and concluding that we're not so bad after all. There is little personal accountability for what we do or don't do. But denying the reality of our sin, or not taking any personal accountability for it, goes against everything we are taught in God's Word. It even contradicts what we see in human nature, beginning as early as infancy.

Still, people don't like to admit they are sinners and might just need forgiveness from a holy God. Yet, before we can be set free from the slavery of our sin, we must acknowledge it exists. It is said that one of the easiest places to share the gospel of Christ is in a prison, because there, people *know* they have sinned. The prison cell is a constant reminder of the inmate's offenses. But for us, no such reminder exists. We have to be aware of our guilt often without any kind of societal indictment. Each of us must come to a place where we recognize our own sin, and realize we are on a crash course with eternal death unless we turn to our loving Savior and accept His free gift of salvation.

> For everyone has sinned; we all fall short of God's glorious standard. (Romans 3:23 NLT)

Sin separates us from God. Although sin is part of our human nature, it goes completely *against* the very nature of God. As we discussed in Chapter Four on the breastplate of righteousness, God is holy, perfect, without sin or fault. Therefore our sin creates a chasm between us and God – a great divide that somehow must be bridged in order for us to be in a healthy, right relationship with our sinless Creator. Without the gift of salvation we will remain in our lost, sinful state – condemned to spend eternity separated from God. That seems like a rather harsh punishment for a condition we are born with, doesn't it? And, I suppose from a human perspective it is. But the fact is, God does not grade on a curve. We were created by a holy, perfect God who cannot have a relationship with sinful man. Yet that is exactly what He wants, an intimate relationship with imperfect people.

Before God created us He knew we would rebel, choosing our own way over His. So in His great love and mercy God provided a way out – salvation through the blood of His Son. Our fallen human nature is and always will be prone to sin as long as we are in these human bodies. But through the free gift of salvation, the punishment for our sin is placed on the sinless shoulders of the righteous One, so we can stand forgiven before the throne of our holy God.

> Surely the arm of the LORD is not too short to save, nor his ear too dull to hear. But your iniquities have separated you from your God; your sins have hidden his face from you, so that he will not hear. (Isaiah 59:1–2)

Salvation Is a Gift

As sinful men and women, there is nothing we can do to earn our salvation. The Bible says unmistakably that it is a gift given by the God who loves us.

Salvation was the plan of a loving God. It never ceases to amaze me that the God who created mankind knew we would turn our backs on Him before He ever made us. He knew we would choose our own pride and selfishness instead of His perfection and glory. Yet He chose to create us anyway, all the while knowing He would have to sacrifice His own Son to set us free from our sin. God Himself did not want to be separated from you and me.

Just think about that. God could have decided not to create us, knowing we would turn away. Or, He could have left us in our sinful state to pay the consequences for our own rebellion. But He chose to do neither. God loved us so much He found a way to reconcile us to Himself so that we could have an intimate relationship with Him for eternity.

From the beginning of time, our God of love had His plan of salvation in mind. Even before He created Adam and Eve, He fashioned His plan to save them and all their descendants by sending His own Son to die in our place. That, my friend, is love. This plan of salvation, created in the mind of our heavenly Father before any of us ever walked the earth, would be His gift to us while we were still in the depths of our sin and depravity. What a God we have!

> It is God who saved us and chose us to live a holy life. He did this not because we deserved it, but because that was his plan long before the world began – to show his love and kindness to us through Christ Jesus. (2 Timothy 1:9 NLT)

Salvation is a gift of God's grace. It has been more than thirty years since I was first overwhelmed by the amazing grace of our God. I can still remember that powerful message. I wrote the illustration my pastor used in the margin of my Bible and although it is fading, it remains written there today. He described grace this way:

God's Riches At Christ's Expense

Salvation comes to us *by means of* grace, *through* faith. We don't deserve to be saved. We don't deserve to be reconciled to a perfect Creator. Yet because of God's unrelenting grace, mercy and love, He has offered us this gift, totally free of charge.

> For it is by grace you have been saved, through faith – and this is not from yourselves, it is the gift of God – not by works, so that no one can boast. (Ephesians 2:8–9)

The gift is free, but oh what a high price was paid by God's own Son! Jesus not only gave up His place in heaven to become a mere human, He did so knowing He would give up that very human life for sinners who would reject Him. Christ willingly accepted the guilt and shame for all of mankind's sin, knowing His Father would have to turn His back, repulsed by the sin His Son had now become. (2 Corinthians 5:21) Jesus graciously did all this so that we, His rebellious children, might be rescued from the chains and punishment of sin. We must never insult God by trying to earn our salvation. It cost Him far too much!

Everything for nothing – An aged saint, on being asked to describe salvation, aptly replied, "Something for nothing." Another aged saint, who had weathered the storms for many a long year and was nearing the heavenly harbor, on hearing this story related, exclaimed, "Yes, it's even better than that. It's everything for nothing." – Grace Robinson[17]

Salvation comes through faith, not by works. If we could earn salvation through our good deeds or obedience to God, then Christ died for nothing. (Galatians 2:21) But, salvation does not come as a result of our works. It is given by the grace of our loving Father, through our faith. We cannot earn it. We cannot work for it. We cannot buy it or bargain for it, and many scholars believe we cannot lose it. We won't debate that question here, as this is a topic that divides entire Christian denominations, and Satan loves that! What we know without a doubt is that salvation is truly a gift from God, which comes to us through our faith in Jesus Christ. That is the clear, indisputable message of the gospel. Let's not let the enemy win by focusing on unanswerable questions; instead, let's focus on the answer – Jesus Christ.

But when the kindness and love of God our Savior appeared, he saved us, not because of righteous things we had done, but because of his mercy. (Titus 3:4-5)

Only Jesus Saves

A drowning person cannot save himself. In order to be rescued, that person must not only be aware of his need and willing to trust the person who has come to save him, but he also needs to give up control.

When my husband was a young boy, he fell through thin ice on a frozen lake near his home. In the pitch black of that ice-cold water, he could not even find the hole he had fallen through in order to call to his friend. He tried desperately to save himself but the more he struggled, the more tired and panic-stricken he became. He lost all sense of direction and couldn't find his way to the top of the water, where he might have discovered the small air pocket between the water and ice that could have provided life-saving oxygen. It was not until he completely gave up that he finally floated to the top of the dark, cold water. He could not save himself. By the grace of God, he was still near the hole in the ice, and his friend grabbed his arm and pulled him to safety.

That story is a perfect illustration of how we should trust our Savior. We need to stop struggling and trying to save ourselves with our insufficient good deeds and acts of self-righteousness. Isaiah 64:6 tells us that "… all our righteous acts are like filthy rags." We are drowning! We cannot be saved until and unless we give up control and trust that the strong hand of our Savior will reach down and pull us to safety in His loving arms.

> Salvation is found in no one else, for there is no other name under heaven given to mankind by which we must be saved. (Acts 4:12)

So much more could be written about God's remarkable gift of salvation. But let's move ahead and look at how Satan tries to pierce our helmet of salvation.

Satan's Schemes Against Salvation

In *The Bible Exposition Commentary*, Warren Wiersbe says, "Satan wants to attack the mind the same way he defeated Eve in the garden (Genesis 3; 2 Corinthians 11:1–3). The helmet refers to the mind controlled by God. It is too bad that many Christians have the idea that the intellect is not important, when in reality it plays a vital role in Christian growth, service, and victory. When God controls the mind, Satan cannot lead the believer astray."[18]

How does Satan try to lead us astray? And what does salvation have to do with "a mind controlled by God?" Because we are God's own children, saved by His grace, our heavenly Father can and does take control of our minds and our lives. But our enemy continues to relentlessly deceive, making us question our own salvation and trying to draw us away from our intimate relationship with God. He uses two obvious deceptive tactics.

Satan tries to make us question our salvation. All of us, believers and unbelievers alike, are born with a sinful nature. It has been part of our human *DNA* since the fall of mankind in the Garden of Eden. When we accept Christ's gift of salvation, we become a new creation. (2 Corinthians 5:17) We are given a new spiritual nature because of our relationship with Jesus Christ. However, as long as we are in these human bodies, our old sin nature (the flesh) and our new nature in Christ (the Spirit) will do battle against each other every single day of our lives.

> The sinful nature wants to do evil, which is just the opposite of what the Spirit wants. And the Spirit gives us desires that are the opposite of what the sinful nature desires. These two forces are constantly fighting each other, so you are not free to carry out your good intentions.
> (Galatians 5:17 NLT)

As believers, even though we sometimes fail and give in to our old sin nature, the truth is Christ defeated sin at the cross. Sin no longer rules us because through Christ's gift of salvation, in the eyes of God, our sin is gone. God doesn't even remember it. (Hebrews 8:12) We will battle against our old nature as long as we live in these earthly bodies, but as God's children we never have to be controlled by sin again.

> But now that you have been set free from sin and have become slaves to God, the benefit you reap leads to holiness, and the result is eternal life. (Romans 6:22)

Christ's once-and-for-all payment for our sin has reconciled us to our holy God. Good deeds could never bridge the gap between sinful man and a holy God. That chasm is far too wide. Only His free gift of salvation can make us children of the King and remove the barrier that once separated us from the God who created us. That is freedom! That is victory!

No wonder Satan works so hard to make us question our very salvation. No wonder he tries to make us think we have to earn our way into God's favor. The enemy knows the truth. He knows it is impossible to be good enough. He knows our acts of righteousness can never unite us with our holy God, which is exactly why he tells us that's what it takes to be saved. If he can get us onto the futile track of self-righteousness and working for our salvation, all he has to do to defeat us is make his stinging accusations every time we fail. And oh yes, make no mistake, we will fail. We are human. Saved, washed by the blood, forgiven children, but in this worldly body, still battling with our old sin nature every day. "If we claim to be without sin, we deceive ourselves and the truth is not in us." (1 John 1:8)

Don't let the enemy deceive you. Your salvation is not dependent upon what you do or don't do. Salvation is a free gift given by God's grace. It is received by faith. It is completely and totally unearned. It can never be taken away from you by anyone or anything. Your sins are forgiven – all of them, past, present and future – removed as far as the east is from the west. (Psalm 103:12) If salvation depended upon our own righteousness no one would be saved, because only Jesus is sinless. (Hebrews 4:15)

God's desire is for us to become more and more like His Son. When we become His children, He gives us the Holy Spirit who works in us throughout our lives to make us more and more like Jesus every day. But when we fail, we don't lose God's love, His gifts or our position as His child. That's the amazing power of God's plan. The price was paid once – for all. "For Christ died for sins once for all, the righteous for the unrighteous, to bring you to God." (1 Peter 3:18) Jesus died for your sins before you even existed. Don't ever forget that His payment is enough.

Satan tells us salvation is a license to sin. There is another way I believe our enemy uses the gift of salvation to pull us away from God. If he cannot make us doubt our salvation, Satan will try to deceive us into thinking our free gift of salvation gives us a license to sin. Nothing could be further from the truth. The forgiveness of sin does not make sin acceptable to God. "What then? Shall we sin because we are not under law but under grace? By no means!" (Romans 6:15)

God hates sin but He loves sinners. He loved us enough to pay the ultimate price to free us from slavery and bondage to sin. He set us free not only for eternal life, but also for freedom in this life. Not freedom to sin, but the freedom that comes from walking away from the chains of sin. Remember, we are freed from our slavery to sin because the Son Himself has set us free. But as long as we are in these human bodies, our old sin nature will be at war with our new nature in Christ. Don't let the enemy deceive you into thinking because you have received the gift of salvation, you can now "enjoy" a life of sin.

Why, after feasting at the table of the King, would you ever want to go back to eating filthy waste in the garbage heap of sin? God will not take away our salvation when we foolishly choose our own sinful way instead of His perfect path. All of our sin has been forgiven. But I can almost hear Him saying, "My child, I have so much more for you. You are royalty! Don't wallow in the garbage of sin any longer. Look, I have a feast for you!"

Let God's Spirit work in your heart to transform you from the inside out. Feast at His table. You only have to say "Yes Lord!"

Putting On the Helmet of Salvation

God has given us the free gift of salvation to wear as a helmet to protect our minds against the enemy's deception and attacks. But just as a physical helmet can't protect a soldier unless he puts it on, our helmet of salvation cannot protect our minds if we do not pick it up and wear it. That can only happen by staying in God's Word and applying it to our lives. Let's look now at how we can put on our helmet every day, protecting our minds against the lies of the accuser.

KNOW you are saved. Have you received the gift of salvation? Does the enemy whisper doubts into your mind and make you question if your decision to follow Jesus was real? If you have accepted Christ as your Savior, you never need to doubt again. God has adopted you as His own child, and nothing can ever separate you from Him. (Romans 8:38–39) Salvation is forever!

And if you have never made the choice to believe and trust Christ for your salvation, you can do it today. This very minute, as you read these words, you can turn to Jesus and make the decision that will reconcile you to your loving Father, and make you His child for eternity.

Jesus told us to come to Him like a little child. Receiving the gift of salvation is so simple, even a child can understand it.

Turn. The biblical name for this is *repentance*, which comes from the Greek word, *metanoia*. It means a change of mind and purpose. The Bible tells us that repentance "leads to salvation." (2 Corinthians 7:10) Before we can believe and trust Christ for our salvation, we first have to recognize that we are sinful and in need of a Savior.

Believe. When we decide to turn to Christ and admit our sinfulness, He offers us His indescribable, free gift of salvation. The website GotQuestions.org gives this beautiful, simple explanation:

"Believe in the Lord Jesus, and you will be saved" (Acts 16:31). God has already done all of the work. All you must do is receive in faith, the salvation God offers (Ephesians 2:8–9). Fully trust in Jesus alone as the payment for your sins. Believe in Him, and you will not perish (John 3:16). God is offering you salvation as a gift. All you have to do is accept it. Jesus is the way of salvation (John 14:6).[19]

Simple. Powerful. Life-changing. The gift of salvation in Christ is yours as soon as you turn and receive it.

REST in your salvation. Once you have turned to Christ and asked Him to forgive your sin, you never have to doubt again. The lies of the enemy, saying you are not good enough, have no power when you know the truth. Your sins are forgiven. This truth will surely set you free.

> But when the kindness and love of God our Savior appeared, he saved us, not because of righteous things we had done, but because of his mercy. (Titus 3:4–5)

DECLARE your salvation. Don't hide your light under a bushel. (Mark 4:21) Let the world know you have received an unbelievable and unearned gift. Tell of the wonderful freedom and peace that is yours through God's gift of salvation. This is the *good news* of the Gospel.

> I do not hide your righteousness in my heart; I speak of your faithfulness and your saving help. I do not conceal your love and your faithfulness from the great assembly. (Psalm 40:10)

The helmet of salvation is all about protecting our minds. We find a perfect example of the power of a mind protected by truth in the classic movie, *The Wizard of Oz*. Shortly after a tornado drops Dorothy's house into the strange and beautiful Land of Oz, killing the Wicked Witch of the East, her sister, the Wicked Witch of the West, appears in a dramatic gust of orange smoke and thunder. She threatens to repay Dorothy for killing her sister and the scared little girl believes the frightening threats, shuddering in fear. Glinda, the Good Witch of the North however, knows the Wicked Witch has no power in Oz and scoffs at her theatrics. Glinda's simple words, "Be gone, you have no power here!" put everything back into perspective and the Wicked Witch of the West leaves the scene, while threatening that she will get Dorothy at a later time.

And so it is with our minds and the helmet of salvation. When Satan begins his growling and chest-beating in your mind, trying to get you to cower to him and believe his lies, just think of Glinda and do what I do. I often speak these words out loud so the enemy and his demons can hear me. "In the name of Jesus and by the power of His blood, be gone. You have no power here!" The enemy will retreat with a whimper until another time. (Luke 4:13) Yes, there will be another time. The battle will continue until we are home in the arms of our Savior.

Salvation – Our Reason for Joy

Rejoice! Your helmet of salvation is a gift worth celebrating. Don't forget to thank God for the joy that is yours in His gift. You have been set free from the chains of sin forever. Amazing joy and peace are yours because God paid the price for your freedom. You truly do have a *future and a hope*. (Jeremiah 29:11)

> Surely this is our God; we trusted in him, and he saved us. This is the Lord, we trusted in him; let us rejoice and be glad in his salvation.
> (Isaiah 25:9)

The Helmet of Salvation – Reflections

Key Takeaway:

> Christ *defeated sin* at the cross. Sin no longer rules us because through Christ's gift of salvation, in the eyes of God, our sin is gone.

Memory Verse:

> "For it is by grace you have been saved, through faith – and this not from yourselves, it is the gift of God." (Ephesians 2:8)

Notes:

The Helmet of Salvation – Study Questions

1. Read 1 Thessalonians 5:8, Isaiah 59:17 and Ephesians 6:17. Our helmet of salvation protects our minds. How can you protect your mind from Satan's lies?

2. Read Romans 7:14–25. Sin is part of our very nature as human beings. If God knew mankind would rebel against him, why do you think He chose to create us anyway?

3. Read John 15:9–17. Jesus Himself calls us His friends. God desires to be in a relationship with you and me. How does it feel to know God wants to be your friend? How do *you* respond?

4. Read John 10:7–10. We know our salvation through Christ assures our eternity with God. But does your salvation affect your everyday life? If so, how? How does being saved give you freedom and victory in your everyday battles?

5. Read Ephesians 2:4–10. Salvation is a gift of God's grace. This passage says the riches of God's grace are expressed in His kindness to us. How has Christ shown His kindness to you? To your family? Make a list and thank Him every day!

8

The Sword of the Spirit

For the word of God is alive and powerful.
It is sharper than the sharpest two-edged sword.
Hebrews 4:12 NLT

Our Only Offensive Weapon

My prayer is that by now you are feeling much more equipped to stand firm against your enemy, the devil. We have come a long way, but we're not quite finished dressing for battle. We've put on the belt of truth, the breastplate of righteousness and the shoes of peace. We've taken up the shield of faith and protected our minds with the helmet of salvation. Now it is time to take up our last piece of battle armor, the *sword of the Spirit*. The sword is our only *offensive* weapon against a formidable enemy. All the other armor God has provided protects us from the attacks of Satan. But with our sword, the Word of God, we can finally do some fighting back!

Just as we have in previous chapters, let's first consider the actual sword the Roman soldiers carried as the apostle Paul reflected on their armor from his prison cell. Then we'll dig deep into what the Bible tells us about our own sword – His Word.

The Ancient Armor – The Warrior's Sword

When we think of a sword, we often picture the long, thin type used in fencing. The Greek word for that kind of sword is *rhomphaia*. But the Greek word used in Ephesians 6:17 is *machaira*, which refers to a short, small dagger.[20] The typical sword of Roman soldiers in New Testament times was a lightweight, well-balanced weapon with a blade about two feet long.[21] The sword was carried

on the soldier's side and hung from the belt or from a leather strap over the shoulder. It was a powerful offensive weapon in the hand of a skilled soldier.  Brandishing it served as an intimidating warning to the enemy.

God's Armor – The Sword of the Spirit

Between the first biblical reference to the sword, the mysterious flaming sword in Genesis 3:24, and the final mention of this weapon, the sword of judgment in Revelation 19:21, the term "sword" appears in the Bible well over four hundred times, making it the most frequently mentioned weapon in Scripture.[22] No wonder the apostle Paul chose the sword to represent the final and only offensive weapon in our battle against "the powers of this dark world." (Ephesians 6:12)

Just like the Roman soldier's sword, the Word of God is a *machaira,* a razor-sharp dagger that, when used decisively, can do considerable damage to the enemy. And like the sword of the Roman soldier in Paul's day, our sword of the Spirit must be brandished boldly to let our enemy know he must stay away – we belong to the King of Kings.

How much do we really know about our powerful offensive weapon, the Word of God? In *How to Study the Bible,* John MacArthur says this about the term *"word"* as it was used in Ephesians 6:17:

> … the Greek word used for "word" in this verse is not logos. Logos is a general word: the Bible is the logos, Christ is the logos, or a general "word" is logos. When the Bible wants to speak of a specific, it uses the word rhema. Now it

means "a specific statement." So the sword of the Spirit is the specific statement of the Word of God that meets the specific point of temptation. Now some people may say, "Well, I have the sword of the Spirit – I own a Bible." Listen, you could own a Bible warehouse, and you wouldn't have the sword of the Spirit. Having the sword of the Spirit is not owning a Bible, but knowing the specific principle in the Bible that applies to the specific point of temptation. The only way Christians will know victory in the Christian life is for them to know the principles of the Word of God so that they can apply them to the specific points where Satan attacks, where the flesh attacks, and where the world attacks. As Christians fill themselves up with the Word of God, it then becomes the source of victory. We can't live the Christian life without studying the Bible. It's the source of truth, it's the source of joy, and it's the source of victory.[23]

Taking up our sword requires more than just a casual knowledge of God's Word. We need to be ready to use God's Word skillfully and intentionally against all of Satan's lies. The enemy knows every one of us and is familiar with all our weaknesses. It is critical that we know the truth of God's Word and how it applies to our own vulnerabilities in order to fight effectively against such a shrewd foe. Let's explore the truth about God's Word and how it will help us fight back against our adversary.

God's Word is truth. We need to look back at this point to our discussion on the belt of truth. Remember, we learned that our belt is worn at all times, both in peace and in battle. This part of our armor holds us firm and allows us to keep all our other weapons right by our side for protection. Our sword, the Word of God, fits right into the belt of truth. It *is* truth. Our enemy's lies are rendered powerless in the light of the truth of God's Word.

> Sanctify them by the truth; your word is truth.
> (John 17:17)

God's Word is powerful. Everything in the universe was created by the power of God's word. (Hebrews 11:3) It is the power of God's Word that pierces a sinful heart, just as a sword pierces the body, and changes lives. It is the power of God's Word – written, spoken and prayed – that defeats the lies of Satan and sends our enemy running in defeat. And it is the power of the WORD of God, Jesus Himself, that defeated Satan forever at the cross of Calvary.

> For the word of God is alive and powerful. It is sharper than the sharpest two-edged sword, cutting between soul and spirit, between joint and marrow. It exposes our innermost thoughts and desires. (Hebrews 4:12 NLT)

God's Word is eternal. The Bible is God's revealed truth, written by mere men over a period of 1500 years. But the truth that God revealed to these writers has existed since eternity past, and will remain into eternity future. There is comfort and assurance in knowing that God's Word, which we use as a piercing dagger against the lies and attacks of our enemy, is timeless. It always was and always will be powerful and effective to defeat our foe. You can count on God's Word today, tomorrow and always.

> The grass withers and the flowers fall, but the word of our God endures forever. (Isaiah 40:8)

God's Word is perfect. There are no mistakes in the Word of God. It is completely flawless. God does not wish He had added or removed anything before it was "published." Satan will try to tell us there are contradictions or inconsistencies in God's Word, or that it is not relevant for current times. You can see the enemy's lies at work today as many in our society seek to re-interpret the Bible – putting it in a "modern" context based upon present-day social values. But the fact is our God has given us His perfect, complete, and timeless Word. Remember, when the enemy puts doubts or confusion in your mind, hold tight to what you know is true. With our limited human minds we will never completely understand the Word of God. But never, ever doubt that the God's Word is perfect, complete and your powerful sword against the enemy.

> All Scripture is God-breathed and is useful for teaching, rebuking, correcting and training in righteousness, so that the servant of God may be thoroughly equipped for every good work.
> (2 Timothy 3:16-17)

God's Word is life. It cleanses. It heals. It is light and life, illuminating truth in a world filled with lies, and giving us the power to live a life filled with purpose and joy. The Holy Spirit uses the Word of God to penetrate our hard hearts and make us more like Christ. The Word of God convicts sinners, changing us into saints. No wonder the enemy wants to pollute the Word by distorting and denying it. Satan comes to steal, kill and destroy, but Christ, THE WORD of God, came to give us life.

> The thief comes only to steal and kill and destroy. I came that they may have life and have it abundantly. (John 10:10)

God's Word is Jesus Christ. Know Jesus and you know truth. Know Jesus and you know life. Know Jesus and you know God. Know Jesus and you know how to defeat His enemy and yours. Jesus is the way, the truth and the life. He is the "Word made flesh." (John 1:14) Jesus is the personification of all God is, in human flesh. He is the One who ultimately defeated Satan. With the Spirit of Jesus Himself living inside you, you have everything you need to fight against our enemy, and win!

> In the beginning was the Word, and the Word was with God, and the Word was God. He was with God in the beginning. Through him all things were made; without him nothing was made that has been made. In him was life, and that life was the light of men. The light shines in the darkness, but the darkness has not understood it. (John 1:1–5)

God's Word is our perfect and powerful sword, always available to defeat the evil one. When Jesus was tempted by Satan in the wilderness, He demonstrated exactly how we should wield the sword of the Spirit to overcome our foe. He used the power and authority of

God's Word to rebuke His enemy. It's incredible how brazen Satan is. Even when he was tempting the very Son of God, he had the audacity to use Scripture to try to defeat Him. Oh how foolish he was, attempting to use God's Word to defeat THE WORD. And he still uses the same tactic with us today.

Just as Satan tries to use our defensive battle armor against us, he will also attempt to defeat us by using our offensive weapon, the Word of God, against us as well. It's time to examine some of his methods.

The Enemy's Methods

It is almost comical to see how the enemy's methods and schemes never seem to change. You'd think he would try something new, but by his very nature he continually resorts to lies, deception and trickery. Obviously, he is very good at it, deceiving millions of people and keeping them far from a loving God. Unless believers are wise enough to put on God's armor, we too can be deceived by the schemes and lies of a very powerful enemy. He uses the same tactics against us that he used against Jesus Himself.

Satan attacks us at our points of vulnerability. When Jesus was tempted by Satan in the desert, He had been fasting for forty days. Remember, Jesus was not only fully God, but he was also fully human, so He was undoubtedly physically weakened by extreme hunger. I don't know about you, but I can't even fast one day without feeling like I'm going to die, much less forty days.

It is not surprising Satan's first fiery arrow was aimed at Jesus' physical need by trying to tempt Him to turn a stone into bread to relieve His hunger. (Luke 4:3) Jesus responded by wielding the sword of the Spirit – the Word of God. He quoted Deuteronomy 8:3 where Moses reminded his people that God had provided manna for them in the desert, and that "man does not live on bread alone but on every word that comes from the mouth of the LORD." Jesus knew God's plan. He took the Father at His Word, and trusted Him for sustenance. Jesus knew He would not die of hunger in the wilderness.

Notice what Satan said, "If you are the Son of God…" I don't think he was trying to make Jesus doubt His identity. Rather, by twisting the truth, he argued that since Jesus *is* the Son of God, He should use His powers to meet His own needs. He uses that argument with us every day. He tells us we are surely capable and even have an obligation and right to take charge of our own lives, to take matters into our own hands and stop depending on someone else – even God. The deceit did not work with Jesus, who defeated it with just the right Scripture to silence the lie.

Be sure you know your areas of vulnerability. Satan does! Know where he will try to lure you into self-sufficiency. Then, be sure you know the truth, and tell yourself the truth, about each and every one of your weaknesses so you too can defeat Satan's lies and temptations with the truth of God's Word.

Satan tempts us with power and pleasure. Satan often attacks us most viciously after a time of blessing. In our Lord's case, it was immediately after His baptism, and following a time of deep communion with His Father. At this time of intense intimacy with God, the enemy tried to get Jesus to reject His Father's plan. In the second temptation of Jesus (Luke 4:5–8), the enemy tempted Jesus to avoid the suffering of the cross and seize an earthly kingdom instead. Remember, Jesus was both God and man, so He may have been tempted with earthly power. After all, most of His followers thought He came to be an earthly king and save the Jewish people from their earthly enemies.

Perhaps it was because Satan knew Jesus' followers wanted Him to be an earthly king that he decided to tempt Jesus with what he thought was his to give … the kingdoms of the world. Satan does have significant power over worldly kingdoms; just look what is happening across the world today. And he claims that the authority and glory of those kingdoms belong to him. Jesus resisted him again, using the power of the Word of God, by quoting Deuteronomy 6:13. "Fear the LORD your God, serve him only."

It's interesting – Jesus never questioned Satan's earthly power. Jesus knew that for now the enemy has been given the power to influence and deceive mankind. For now. Satan tempts us with the same lures of power, control over our own lives, and avoidance of pain and suffering if we would just deny God and do life his way. He knows what our weak flesh needs and how to offer us things that seem, oh, so sweet. Let's always look to Jesus' own example and fight back with the sword of the Spirit.

Satan twists the Word of God. Satan knows Scripture. He is a master at misrepresenting and distorting God's Word in order to accomplish his own evil purposes. In the third temptation of Jesus (Luke 4:9–12) Satan quoted part of Psalm 91 in an attempt to get Jesus to jump from the highest point of the temple.

> For he will command his angels concerning you to guard you in all your ways; they will lift you up in their hands, so that you will not strike your foot against a stone. (Psalm 91:11–12)

But, curiously, the enemy chose *not* to quote the very next verse which speaks of his own fate!

You will tread upon the lion and the cobra; you
will trample the great lion and the serpent.
(Psalm 91:13)

Satan wanted Jesus to test God's promise of protection. But once again Jesus' response was to fight the
deception of the enemy with the sword of the Spirit, the
truth of Scripture. Jesus quoted Deuteronomy 6:16. "Do
not put the LORD your God to the test." Jesus refused
to test the faithfulness and protection of His Father.

The enemy will always mislead us, trying to make us
think the Word of God says something it really doesn't.
That is why it is extremely important for us to understand
God's Word and the principles it teaches. Some people
say we can find passages to make the Word of God say
anything we want it to say. That is what Satan counts on.
But distortion like that only works if you take verses out
of context, leave out words, or try to apply things to
Christians that were never meant to pertain to us, just as
the enemy does. The better you know the Word of God,
the easier it will be for you to recognize and reject Satan's
lies.

Satan returns at opportune times. After Jesus wrestled
with the temptations of Satan in the desert, He must have
been exhausted. Two of the three gospel accounts of
Jesus' temptation (Matthew and Mark) tell us that after

Satan left Jesus, angels came and attended Him. Isn't it wonderful to know these same ministering spirits who tended to Jesus when He was weak in His humanity, will also minister to us in our weakness and temptation as well? (Hebrews 1:14)

In Luke's gospel account of Jesus' temptation he adds something the other two writers don't regarding what happened after Jesus' wrestling match with Satan. Luke tells us: "When the devil had finished all this tempting, he left him until an opportune time." (Luke 4:13) Pretty unmistakable isn't it? Satan will be back. He looks for opportune times. He will likely wait until you are at your weakest point, whether from illness, stress or simply exhaustion. You may be particularly vulnerable because you've just come out of a wonderful time of refreshing or blessing and you are feeling just a bit too self-confident. Or maybe you have wandered too close to temptation, either purposely or by accident. The enemy waits for the perfect time to come around again. And make no mistake, he will be back.

Picking Up the Sword of the Spirit

Now it's our turn. After all the defensive armor we so diligently and obediently put on, it's time for us to pick up our sword. As we said earlier in this chapter, our sword of the Spirit is not a large swashbuckling sword like the one Captain Jack Sparrow used in *Pirates of the Caribbean*. It's a personal weapon, a dagger. We must learn to use it decisively and very specifically against the attacks the enemy is launching at us personally. And remember, this is a spiritual battle. We must fight our spiritual enemies with spiritual weapons. (2 Corinthians 10:4) The Word of God is the best spiritual weapon we can possibly have. It has life and power (Hebrews 4:12) and never grows dull. We can conquer our enemy as we understand God's Word, memorize it and obey it. Let's look at some of the specific ways we can use our sword effectively against our forceful enemy.

Know the Word of God. It is essential that we know the truths of God's Word. Study Scripture; don't just memorize verses. Of course, having the right verse at our fingertips, or on the tip of our tongue, is a critical element in fighting back against the enemy. But it doesn't help to know the Scripture verses unless you understand the biblical principles behind the passages and how to apply them. Don't follow the enemy's example and simply take verses out of context, trying to make them fit whatever you want them to fit. You must seek to learn what God was teaching when He inspired the writers of Scripture to pen these powerful words. You must understand the writers' meaning in the context of the consistent message of Scripture as well as the historical and societal norms of the time in which it was written. Then you will be able to discern how the Scripture applies to *your* life and the specific areas where the enemy will tempt you or lie to you.

Seems like a lot of work, right? But we have a powerful and loving God. He will honor your desire and effort to obey Him by teaching you and giving you *what* you need *when* you need it to fight your battles. Remember, this is war. Don't think you can just rush off into battle wearing your sweat suit and gym shoes. Put on your armor. Take up the sword of the Spirit. The Word of God is powerful and effective, a mighty weapon available for us in our daily battles. Make the sword your own. Use it wisely, decisively, correctly and efficiently. It will send your enemy running.

> For the word of God is alive and active. Sharper than any double-edged sword, it penetrates even to dividing soul and spirit, joints and marrow; it judges the thoughts and attitudes of the heart. (Hebrews 4:12)

Spot the enemy's lies. Many Christians make the mistake of getting all their biblical knowledge from other people, or from just one teacher. Oh, don't get me wrong, it's extremely important to sit under the teaching of good Bible teachers. But men and women are humans. We are all fallible. We can and do get things wrong. And there are probably as many opinions on Scripture as there are fast-food restaurants in the city of Atlanta. It is your responsibility to know the truth of God's Word yourself. Then when someone gives you his or her opinion on something in the Bible, or you hear a sermon that just doesn't sound right to you, you will be able to discern the truth. The Bible tells us to be wise as serpents and gentle as doves. (Matthew 10:16) It also warns us to be careful of deceiving spirits. (1 John 4:1) Don't rely totally on what others teach. Do your homework! In this day and age of the Internet and unlimited free resources, there is no reason you can't read the same Bible commentaries and studies your pastor uses to write his sermons. Then, after you've done your homework, go talk to your pastor or someone with good theological training and ask questions. Seek the truth. God is found by all who earnestly seek Him. (Proverbs 8:17)

When I was a young girl being raised by devout Catholic parents, a large Bible sat on the table in our living room, but no one ever read it. I was a curious little girl and frequently looked at the pictures. As I grew older, I wondered why we didn't read this big, beautiful book that graced our table. My father told me that "lay people" were not educated enough to interpret the Bible. He said only the priests had enough knowledge and training to understand what it meant, so we were to learn from them. How sad! Even back in the days before the Internet, the power and truth of the Word of God pierced the hearts of all those who studied it.

Today, with the same tools used by ministers, priests and Bible teachers available to you online, don't miss out! Devour the Word. Study it. Learn it yourself. Ask questions and then ask God to give you the discernment you need to recognize when you are hearing a lie from the enemy or from one of his well-disguised workers.

> Dear friends, do not believe everyone who claims to speak by the Spirit. You must test them to see if the spirit they have comes from God. For there are many false prophets in the world. (1 John 4:1 NLT)

Pray the Word. God's Word and our direct access to God through prayer are weapons against which Satan is powerless. Remember, the enemy wants to separate us from God, and his primary method is to fill our minds with lies. But when we know the truth of God's Word, we can defeat the enemy's lies every time.

So how do we effectively use the Word of God when the enemy fills our minds with twisted, deceitful thoughts? What do we do when perhaps we have allowed Satan to lie to us so long that he has a stronghold in some area of our life, and it seems almost impossible to break free from his deception? Perhaps the area you struggle with is doubt, or pride, or maybe insecurity, or sexual addiction. There are so many places in our lives where the enemy can fill our minds with lies that begin to *own* us.

When we fight the stubborn lies of the enemy, or perhaps lies we have told ourselves from childhood, the most powerful weapons we can use are the Word of God and prayer. There is supernatural power in all kinds of prayer, but when we pray Scripture, God's truth not only exposes the enemy's lies, forcing him to flee, but the truth also becomes unmistakable to us, changing the very way we think as we pray. Praying Scripture is one of the most effective ways to *take every thought captive to obey Christ.* (2 Corinthians 10:5) In Beth Moore's book, *Praying God's Word,* she says this:

> In praying Scripture, I not only find myself in intimate communication with God, but my mind is being retrained, or renewed (Romans 12:2), to think His thoughts about my situation rather than mine. Ultimately, He resumes His proper place in my thought life as huge and indomitable, and my obstacle shrinks.[24]

When we pray God's Word, we focus on God and on His truth, which destroys the enemy's plans and schemes and transforms our minds. How do we pray the Word of God? One way is by taking a verse of Scripture and rewriting it in our own words. This is an example from my own personal prayer journal:

"Lord, you have been our dwelling place throughout all generations." (Psalm 90:1)

Since the day You created mankind Lord, You meant for us to be at "home" anywhere, no matter what house, no matter what city or state or country for that matter, because home is not a place. It's where we live. And we live In You! You are my home. Even if we end up selling and buying and moving ten more times before You take us to eternity, it matters not because I am home – here, at work, in my house, in a hospital, in a store. I am home – I live in YOU.

Another way to pray the Word of God is to meditate on what a particular verse says to you. I thought I'd give you another example from one of my prayer journals. I left it very much as it was originally written so it's in rough form, but hopefully that will be of some benefit to you. And remember, your thoughts don't need to be as verbose as mine are here. God must have been preparing me to be a writer, even back then. Your prayers can be as simple as one or two sentences. God doesn't care. He just loves to hear your voice! He loves that you desire to pray His Word and meet with Him in any way that fits who *you* are.

"May the God of hope fill you with all joy and peace as you trust in Him, so that you may overflow with hope by the power of the Holy Spirit." (Romans 15:13)

Wow! That is exactly what I need. I want joy and peace! I need to overflow with hope. God, I don't want to hang on to it like a slippery fish trying to swim away from me, slipping through my fingers every time I get close. I want to be overflowing with hope! I love that word – overflowing. It means you have so much you just can't contain it all. Of course in this world the first thing people want to be overflowing with is money, though that is so temporary, so meaningless. Wouldn't we all be better off overflowing with laughter, or kindness or joy or yes – please – overflowing with hope? I'm tired of hanging on to hope for dear life.

And this passage says You are the God of hope. What does that mean ... you are the "God of something"? You are the God of love – Love is who You are – it's what You are about. It is intrinsic to your personality. You cannot have anything to do with things that are not done or about or engulfed in or around love. You are the "God of gods," the highest of the high. Nothing is above You. The most powerful forces of this world and the entire universe bow to Your awesomeness and power as You dwarf them to mere specs by your power and majesty. So when we say you are the God of hope, I would think that means without You there is NO hope. You are hope. You are our reason to hope. You give all things a reason to exist, a meaningful existence, a hope for a purpose and a future. You provide the assurance of a tomorrow to hope for. You provide the all-encompassing, never changing, never ending love to hope in. And because of who You are, the God of hope, the one reason for hope, we can receive joy and peace from You, being filled by You with joy and peace.

But here's our part. This passage says "… as you trust in Him". We can't know You as the God of hope until we choose to trust You. You don't always give us miraculous events that shout "Look what I've done! – Trust Me now!" Sometimes, probably most of the time, You simply allow the events in our lives to take their natural course and say to us, "Trust me with the outcome, no matter what it is – good or bad, difficult or easy. Trust Me for the results. I will carry you through and I will grow you and I will use you and I will honor your faithfulness and I will give you whatever you need for whatever I allow you to experience. So … Trust Me … I love you far more than you will ever know!" What a wonderful reason to be overflowing with hope!

The Word of God – Our Source of Joy

The Word of God is a love story, the story of a devoted Father pursuing a rebellious child, who turns from Him time and time again. Yet in His great love, God never gives up. God's Word is the story of the hope, the peace and the joy that are found when we, His disobedient children, finally surrender and say "yes" to the love and grace of our Father. There is joy at every turn in the Word of God. Even through the Old Testament when God was angry with His people and punished them for turning away from Him, there was joy in God's gracious forgiveness, taking back His stubborn children over and over and over again. And the joy that is ours as a result of the plan of salvation, the very Son of God coming to take our shame and guilt, is beyond comprehension.

When we know the Word, study the Word, live the Word, and pray the Word, we can't help but rejoice in the amazing love of the Father who gives unceasingly and forgives unconditionally. Hold on to your sword – God's Word – and understand its power and protection. Shout for joy in the amazing truth of everything you read, everything you learn, and most of all, rejoice in the

WORD, your precious loving Savior, your Source of life and joy.

The Sword of the Spirit – Reflections

Key Takeaway:

Having the sword of the Spirit is not owning a Bible, but knowing the specific principle in the Bible that applies to our specific point of temptation.

Memory Verse:

"Your word is a lamp to my feet and a light for my path." (Psalm 119:105)

Notes:

The Sword of the Spirit – Study Questions

1. Read Ephesians 6:17 and Hebrews 4:12. The sword of the Spirit is our only offensive weapon in this battle with Satan. What do you think it is about God's Word that makes it so powerful?

2. Why is it important to do more than just memorize Scripture? How does knowing the principles of the Bible help you wield God's Word as your sword?

3. Read Luke 4:9–13. Satan's lies frequently twist the truth of Scripture or take it out of context. How does understanding the context of the verses you read, study and memorize help you fight Satan's lies?

4. For each of the four ways Satan tempted Jesus, write a little about how he uses that same method to tempt you.

   - Satan attacks at a point of vulnerability.
   - Satan tempts with power and control.
   - Satan twists and misuses the Word of God.
   - Satan returns at opportune times.

5. How well do you know the Word of God? What is missing in your knowledge or understanding?

6. Have you ever prayed the Word? Practice now. Take your *favorite* verse from this lesson and rewrite it in your own words.

9

The Cover of Prayer

Be joyful always; pray continually;
give thanks in all circumstances,
for this is God's will for you in Christ Jesus.
1 Thessalonians 5:15–18

Our Protective Covering

In this war we fight day after day against the powers of darkness, the battle gear we need to stay protected is not our own – it comes from God. Every piece of our spiritual armor is a gift, provided by a loving Father to help us fight and win our battle against Satan himself. On our own we are no match for the enemy. But *in Christ*, wearing His armor, we have all we need for victory. However, to remain in Christ we need to stay close to Him. That is why, before the apostle Paul ends his instruction on fighting against our formidable enemy, he says "And pray in the Spirit on all occasions with all kinds of prayers and requests. With this in mind, be alert and

always keep on praying for all the Lord's people."
(Ephesians 6:18)

Prayer is the final protective covering in our spiritual
armor. It is a lifeline connecting us to our only source of
power, the provider of each of our spiritual weapons,
Jesus Himself. In Christ we are able to stand against the
schemes of the devil, and prayer anchors us in Christ.
Prayer is powerful. Prayer is necessary. Prayer is a gift.
What an honor and privilege we are given by our loving
Savior who says "Come to me all who are weary ..."
(Matthew 11:28)

Paul tells us to pray on *all occasions*, with *all kinds* of
prayers. He knows it's not enough just to spend a few
minutes offering God a quick prayer at the start of the
day. To fight a battle with a foe as powerful and deceptive
as Satan, we are going to need to stay connected
continuously to the One who gives us power and
protection. Paul reminds us to *stay alert*. We can't afford
to get lazy in war. We must not give the enemy any
opportunity to deceive us with his lies and schemes. And
Paul teaches us to pray not just for ourselves, but for all
the saints. Remember you're not in this battle alone.
Every person who calls Jesus his or her Lord is fighting
right alongside of you. Covering yourself and others in
the protection of prayer is vital. We dare not end our
study without talking about the power, the purpose and
the practice of prayer.

The Power of Prayer

Without our intimate connection to God through prayer, we are standing on our own – open, vulnerable and unprotected. We can desire and even attempt to put on His spiritual armor, but until we connect with God, until we make Christ Himself our armor, all the battle gear we have studied is just a set of tools sitting in God's arsenal, far outside our reach. Unless we connect to the power of the Almighty through prayer, we may as well be trying to turn on a smartphone with a dead battery. There simply is no power.

Power to clothe ourselves in Christ and the sustaining power we need to put on God's armor each day come by remaining, or abiding, in Christ. In John 15:5-6 Jesus said, "I am the vine; you are the branches. If you remain in me and I in you, you will bear much fruit; apart from me you can do nothing." Through prayer, we remain connected to "the Vine" and receive Christ's power and strength. Through the very act of prayer itself, an intimate, ongoing conversation with our Father God, the enemy is kept at bay. When Jesus' name is on our lips and in our hearts; when our every thought is taken captive to Christ through constant interaction with Him; when we draw so close that nothing can pull us away; then we are *covered* in Christ and protected from the flaming arrows of the enemy.

Drawing near to God in prayer protects us from Satan's schemes. It strengthens us so we can put on every piece of God's armor and fight the battle to win. When we are covered and cover others in prayer, we can walk in strength, peace and victory because this war we fight has already been won. We are walking in the power of the victorious Savior!

The Purpose of Prayer

Prayer in the life of a Christian is not optional. All throughout Scripture God commands us to pray. Through prayer we connect intimately with our heavenly Father. This divine relationship is the very purpose of prayer. God is, by His very nature as three persons in one, a relational being who desires to have an intimate relationship with you. Think about that. He longs for you. He loves to hear your voice. He misses you when you stay away. It is not an obligation to pray; it is the highest honor God can give to those He loves.

In the Old Testament, only the high priest was allowed to draw near to God. Once a year he would enter the Most Holy Place behind the veil of the temple to stand before God. (Hebrews 9:7) Having made a sacrifice for himself and for the people, he then brought the blood into the Holy of Holies and sprinkled it on the mercy seat, God's "throne" (Leviticus 16:14–15). He did this to make atonement for himself and the people for all their sins committed during the year just ended (Exodus 30:10).[25]

But now, through Christ's death and resurrection the barrier is removed. Our sin, which kept us from drawing close to God, is gone. Our loving Father longed to be united once again to the children He created. And because of Christ's work on our behalf, God invites us to freely come into His presence, into the true Holy of Holies. What a privilege. What a joy!

This honor is ours not only when we come to God in formal prayer; we are invited to come before His throne on all occasions with all kinds of prayers and requests. That means inviting God into every part of our lives. It is through continual interaction with our heavenly Father that we are protected and given all we need to fight against the schemes of the enemy. But how do we stay this close to God when our lives are so busy and so many things vie for our attention? The most important thing to do is to decide to make being with God a priority. Schedule an appointment each day that you simply will not miss, a time when you can sit down, open God's Word and just talk with Him. This kind of intentional quiet time with God is precious and powerful. Extending intentionality about prayer to moments throughout the day is just as precious and powerful.

If we make prayer a priority, we will find there are many occasions for communicating with God.

In 1 Thessalonians 5:17 Paul tells us to *pray continually* or *pray without ceasing*. Pray before you set your feet on the floor in the morning and when you are getting ready for your day. Pray while driving in the car, as you are doing mundane chores and before you go to sleep at night. Talk to God throughout your day – when you have a difficult decision to make, when you are in the midst of an argument, when you don't know what to say to someone, when you want to say something negative, when you're afraid. When you make prayer a lifestyle, and it becomes a part of your every day, watch and see what God can do!

The Practice of Prayer

Never forget, God is all about relationship. He longs for us to come and have a real, heartfelt conversation with Him. He invites us to pour out our hearts and lay our burdens at his feet. (1 Peter 5:7) But have you ever noticed the conversations we have with God often sound more like a formal speech or a wish list for our fairy godmother than a conversation with an intimate friend? We start our prayers by saying, "Dear God," as if writing a letter to a distant aunt. Or we begin every other sentence with His name, as though God forgot we were talking to Him.

Now, don't get me wrong. God does not care how many times you say Lord, or if you start your prayers by saying "Dear God." He loves to hear your voice no matter what you say or how you say it. But the truth is, He longs for us to simply pour our hearts out to Him. He wants us to come to Him just the way we are, no matter what pain, anger, doubt or fear might be going on in us. Jesus said, "Come to me, all you who are weary and burdened, and I will give you rest." (Matthew 11:28) He invites us to lay our burdens at His feet – at the foot of the cross where He paid the ultimate price so we would never have to hide our hearts again! I remember during one particularly *real* conversation with God, I came to the freeing awareness that He knew exactly what I was thinking. So if I was honest and actually said it, or perhaps was even brave enough to write it in my journal, God was not going to be shocked or appalled. He truly loves us *that* much!

This kind of open dialogue with God is called conversational prayer. But Paul told us to pray with *all* kinds of prayers. And there are many other types of prayer to help us to draw closer to our loving God. Let's look at just a few.

Listening Prayer. A conversation is a two way exchange, so conversational prayer is not complete until we listen to God. Listening Prayer is simply asking God to speak to you, and then writing down what you "hear" Him saying in your heart. I discovered this type of prayer quite by accident during a very difficult time in my life. As I poured out my heart to God in my prayer journal every day, I found that often, the words I wrote were no longer my words to God, but instead they became God's words to me. What I heard my Abba Father say to me during those times was truly a sweet, personal, and life-giving gift! Since that time, I have learned that many others have also discovered the power and joy of this kind of intentional listening prayer. If we ask God to speak to us in faith, He will. He is faithful. He loves to speak to His children.

Are you skeptical? Are you worried that you will only hear or write your own thoughts? Do you think God only speaks to us through His Word? I would encourage you to give listening prayer a try and test what you hear. Check everything God "writes" to you against the truth of Scripture. If anything you heard does not line up with God's Word, you will know it was not from Him. But I assure you, what I and so many others have experienced during these times of listening prayer is that God truly does speak to His children. By intentionally writing what we hear, we give written form to things God was always speaking in our hearts. Try it! You may be surprised by what He says to you.

Intercessory Prayer. Paul concluded his instruction to us on spiritual battle with this final command: "… always keep on praying for all the Lord's people." Praying on behalf of another person is called intercessory prayer. When a Christian comes before the throne of God to pray for the needs of another, he enters a spiritual battle zone. Intercessory prayer takes place in the spiritual world where the battles for our own lives, our families, our friends and our nation are won or lost.[26] The Bible tells us the Spirit of God intercedes for us when we don't know what or how to pray. "In the same way, the Spirit helps us in our weakness. We do not know what we ought to pray for, but the Spirit himself intercedes for us through wordless groans." (Romans 8:26)

As followers of Christ we also have the honor and responsibility to intercede – to pray in another person's place when he or she is in need, or even unable or unwilling to pray. How amazing that God asks us to do for others, just what the Holy Spirit does for us – to enter into God's presence and make intercession for a loved one. This is one of the greatest privileges we have as children of God.

Meditation. Meditation is communicating with God by concentrating and focusing our thoughts on Him. When we meditate on God, our very thoughts become a prayer. Psalm 119:148 says, "My eyes stay open through the watches of the night, that I may meditate on your promises." The practice of meditation is mentioned more than thirty-five times in the Bible. Although the New Age movement and other non-Christian religions have made meditation into something that is far from a godly practice, when the focus of our meditation is on God Himself, His Word, His promises, His deeds or His commands, it then becomes truly an act of worship and prayer, drawing us close to our Father. One very effective way I have found to meditate on God's Word is to rewrite a Psalm or other biblical passage in my own words. It makes Scripture become very personal, and God's Word actually becomes our prayer.

Remember, our method of prayer is not as important as our motive. God is far more interested in our hearts than our words or technique. By telling us to pray with *all kinds of prayers* the apostle Paul is reminding us that we can communicate with our Father God in many ways. Some people have deep, heartfelt conversations with the Lord in the privacy of their own thoughts, while others pray by writing their prayers in a journal. Some pray by reading an inspirational poem or prayer written by someone else and then embracing and offering it to God as their own. There are those who pray in their own private prayer language, or tongues, and others who pray by singing. God is pleased with all of these and more. He smiles whenever our earnest desire is to draw near to Him.

Finally, let's look a little more closely at what it means to "pray in the Spirit." In Ephesians 6:18 Paul instructs us to "Pray *in the Spirit* on all occasions ..." But what exactly is praying in the Spirit? The website GotQuestions.org, a great resource for anyone with questions about the Christian faith, answers this way:

> The Greek word translated "pray in" can have several different meanings. It can mean "by means of," "with the help of," "in the sphere of," and "in connection to." Praying in the Spirit does not refer to the words we are saying. Rather, it refers to how we are praying. Praying in the Spirit is praying according to the Spirit's leading. It is praying for things the Spirit leads us to pray for. Romans 8:26 says, "In the same way, the Spirit helps us in our weakness. We do not know what we ought to pray for, but the Spirit Himself intercedes for us with groans that words cannot express."[27]

Respected Bible teacher and author Dr. Warren W. Wiersbe explains "The Bible formula is that we pray to the Father, through the Son, and in the Spirit. Romans 8:26–27 tells us that only in the Spirit's power can we pray in the will of God. Otherwise, our praying could be selfish and out of the will of God."[28]

Clothed for Battle

Covered in the protection and power of prayer, we are now clothed in Christ and fully armed for battle. Resting in the peace and intimacy of prayer, our journey together ends in a most joyful place – at the feet of Jesus.

> As Jesus and his disciples were on their way, he came to a village where a woman named Martha opened her home to him. She had a sister called Mary, who sat at the Lord's feet listening to what he said. But Martha was distracted by all the preparations that had to be made. She came to him and asked, "Lord, don't you care that my sister has left me to do the work by myself? Tell her to help me!" "Martha, Martha," the Lord answered, "you are worried and upset about many things, but few things are needed – or indeed only one. Mary has chosen what is better, and it will not be taken away from her."
> (Luke 10:38–42)

Oh how I pray that each and every one of us will choose what is better – to sit at Christ's feet – to draw close in worship when we might otherwise worry, to listen when we might ignore, to rest when we might otherwise "do." We will find power, peace and the joy of an intimate relationship at the feet of Jesus.

In this battle that will continue to rage as long as we are in these human bodies, cling to the One who clothes you in Himself. Sit at His feet. Stay so close to Christ that the enemy can't get near enough to touch you. Clothe yourself in Christ and put on His armor every day. He is your hope and your salvation, your victory and your assurance of *Joy in the Battle*.

The Cover of Prayer – Reflections

Key Takeaway:

Prayer is the final protective covering in our spiritual armor. It is a lifeline, connecting us to our only Source of power, Jesus Himself.

Memory Verse:

"Devote yourselves to prayer, being watchful and thankful." (Colossians 4:2)

Notes:

The Cover of Prayer – Study Questions

1. Read Ephesians 6:18. Why do you think Paul tells us to pray on all occasions with all kinds of prayers? What does this tell you about prayer's role in our battle?

2. What keeps you from spending more time with the Lord in prayer? What gets in the way? What can you do to overcome that obstacle?

3. Read Mark 9:25–29. What role has prayer played in *your* battle with the lies and schemes of the enemy? What do you need to do differently to allow prayer to be a powerful weapon in your battle?

4. Read Acts 1:14. The believers in the early church joined together in prayer. What is the advantage in praying with other believers? What else does God's Word tell us about that? (See Matthew 18:20.)

5. Read James 5:14–18. These verses clearly tell us prayer is effective – it *does* something. What does an *effective* prayer look like to you?

6. Many years ago I asked God to help me put on His armor by praying Ephesians 6:10-18 as my own "Battle Prayer." You can download a copy at www.joyonpurpose.com/battle-prayer/. Ask God to help you put on His armor. On a separate sheet of paper, write your own Ephesians 6 prayer.

7. How do you feel about having unlimited access to the God of the universe?

About the Author

MARY SORRENTINO is a Certified Professional Life Coach, author, speaker and founder of *Joy on Purpose Life Coaching.* Mary has been building into people's lives through coaching, mentoring and teaching for over twenty years, helping people find the joy God promises even in the midst of life's most difficult circumstances.

Mary has been married for 38 years to her husband Paul, and has one beautiful daughter, Sarah, and a wonderful son-in-law, Ted. Mary and her family have lived in the Atlanta, Georgia area since 1998.

Mary is the author of two books, *Joy in the Battle,* available now, and *Joy on Purpose* which is scheduled for publication in early 2017. She is also working on additional titles so watch for more additions to the *Joy on Purpose Books* library.

To learn more about Mary's ministry, life coaching, virtual or in-person group Bible studies, or to have Mary speak to your church group or retreat on *Joy in the Battle* or one of her other *Joy on Purpose* topics, visit her website at www.JoyonPurpose.com.

NOTES

Chapter 1

[1] Ingram, Chip. (2006). *The Invisible War.* (p.39). Grand Rapids, Mich.: Baker Books.

[2] Wood, D.R.W., & Marshall, I.H. (1996). *New Bible dictionary* (3rd ed.) (p. 615). Leicester, England; Downers Grove, Ill.: InterVarsity Press.

[3] Walvoord, J.F., Zuck, R.B., & Dallas Theological Seminary. (1983). *The Bible knowledge commentary : An exposition of the scriptures* (Da 10:12–14). Wheaton, Ill.: Victor Books.

[4] Wiersbe, W. W. (1996). *The Bible exposition commentary* (Eph 6:10). Wheaton, Ill.: Victor Books.

[5] Ingram, Chip. (2006). *The Invisible War.* (p. 43). Grand Rapids, Mich.: Baker Books.

Chapter 2

[6] Calvin, J. (1997). *Institutes of the Christian Religion.* Bellingham, Wash.: Logos Research Systems, Inc.

[7] Easton, M. (1996). *Easton's Bible Dictionary.* Oak Harbor, Wash: Logos Research Systems, Inc.

Chapter 3

[8] Hobbs, H.H. (1990). *My Favorite Illustrations* (p. 261). Nashville, Tenn.: Broadman Press.

Chapter 5

[9] Achtemeier, P.J., Harper & Row, P., & Society of Biblical Literature. (1985). *Harper's Bible Dictionary* (1st ed.) (p. 355). San Francisco: Harper & Row.

[10] Swanson, J. (1997). *Dictionary of Biblical Languages with Semantic Domains : Greek (New Testament)* (electronic ed.). Oak Harbor, Wash.: Logos Research Systems, Inc.

[11] Douglas, J. D. (1996). Fear. In D. R. W. Wood, I. H. Marshall, A.R. Millard, J. I. Packer, & D. J. Wiseman (Eds.), *New Bible dictionary* (3rd ed., p. 365). Leicester, England; Downers Grove, Ill.: InterVarsity Press.

[12] Lewis, C.S. (2009). *The Problem of Pain*. C.S. Lewis Signature Classics. New York, NY: HarperCollins Publishers.

[13] Young, Sarah. (2004). "February 13." *Jesus Calling: Enjoying Peace in His Presence: Devotions for Every Day of the Year*. (p. 46). Nashville: Thomas Nelson.

Chapter 6

[14] Knowles, A. (2001). *The Bible Guide* (1st Augsburg books ed.) (p. 622). Minneapolis, Minn.: Augsburg.

[15] Wiersbe, W.W. (1996). *Be Available*. An Old Testament Study. (pp. 58–59). Wheaton, Ill: Victor Books.

Chapter 7

[16] Manser, M.H. (1999). *Dictionary of Bible Themes: The Accessible and Comprehensive Tool for Topical Studies.* London: Martin Manser.

[17] Tan, P.L. (1996). *Encyclopedia of 7700 Illustrations: Signs of the Times.* Garland, Texas: Bible Communications, Inc.

[18] Wiersbe, W.W. (1996). *The Bible Exposition Commentary* (Eph 6:13). Wheaton, Ill.: Victor Books.

[19] Got Questions Ministries, "How can I be saved?" http://www.gotquestions.org/how-can-I-be-saved.html

Chapter 8

[20] MacArthur, J., Jr. (1996). *How to Study the Bible.* John MacArthur's Bible Studies. Chicago: Moody Press.

[21] Achtemeier, P.J., Harper & Row, P., & Society of Biblical Literature. (1985). *Harper's Bible Dictionary* (1st ed.) (pp. 1002–1003). San Francisco: Harper & Row.

[22] Achtemeier, P.J., Harper & Row, P., & Society of Biblical Literature. (1985). *Harper's Bible Dictionary* (1st ed. (p. 1003). San Francisco: Harper & Row.

[23] MacArthur, J., Jr. (1996). *How to Study the Bible.* John MacArthur's Bible Studies. Chicago: Moody Press.

[24] Moore, Beth. (2009). *Praying God's Word.* Nashville, Tenn.:B&H Publishing Group.

Chapter 9

[25] Got Questions Ministries, "What was the biblical role of the high priest?" http://www.gotquestions.org/high-priest.html#ixzz3XUNMKxMm

[26] The Christian Broadcasting Network; "What Is Intercession?" http://www.cbn.com/spirituallife/cbnteachingsheets/keys-intercession.aspx

[27] Got Questions Ministries, "What is praying in the Spirit?" http://www.gotquestions.org/praying-Spirit.html#ixzz3XsCEoWL5

[28] Wiersbe, W.W. (1996). *The Bible exposition commentary* (Vol. 2, p. 60). Wheaton, Ill.: Victor Books.